BREAKING BARRIERS

BREAKING BARRIERS

1 Corinthians
and
Christian Community

LYLE D. VANDER BROEK

Wipf & Stock
PUBLISHERS
Eugene, Oregon

Wipf and Stock Publishers
199 W 8th Ave, Suite 3
Eugene, OR 97401

Breaking Barriers
1 Corinthians and Christian Community
By Vander Broek, Lyle D.
Copyright © 2002 by Vander Broek, Lyle D.
ISBN 13: 978-1-55635-557-8
ISBN 10: 1-55635-557-2
Publication date 7/23/2007
Previously published by Brazos, 2002

To my mother, Alma Popma Vander Broek
and
my father, Robert Vander Broek
and
my stepmother, Alice Foreman Vander Broek

Those whose love continues to shape my
understanding of
Christian community.

Contents

Acknowledgments

Some of the material in this volume is adapted from previously published articles. Interested readers may want to consult these periodicals to see how the biblical texts were used to address somewhat different theological issues. "Community and Christian Leaders" is adapted from "The Art of Listening to Sermons," *Perspectives: A Journal of Reformed Thought* 14/3 (1999): 6–9. "Community and Ethical Boundaries" is adapted from "Discipline and Community: Another Look at 1 Corinthians 5," *Reformed Review* 48/1 (1994): 5–13.

I would like to express my deep appreciation to the University of Dubuque Theological Seminary for granting me two consecutive fall sabbaticals (1997 and 1998), thus making the research for and writing of this volume possible. I would also like to thank various individuals who graciously involved themselves in this project: Dr. Thomas A. Boogaart and Dr. James L. Bailey, who read the manuscript closely and offered numerous suggestions for improvement in its substance and style; my UDTS students, especially my teaching assistant James D. Gunn, who offered invaluable assistance in proofreading; and my secretary Luann LeConte, who patiently edited and shaped the manuscript. Thank you also to Rodney Clapp of Brazos for his steady encouragement throughout the long project.

I am particularly appreciative to my colleagues at the University of Dubuque Theological Seminary for their friendship and support, and to my family, especially my wife Rachel, whose patience and love undergirds all that I do.

Lyle D. Vander Broek

Introduction

A Crisis of Community

Because Christian community is about relationships, one way to determine its vitality is simply to measure Christians' willingness to gather together. Various surveys show that since the early 1960s, church attendance in the United States has fallen by 10–12 percent, and involvement in other forms of church social life (Bible study groups, socials, educational programs, etc.) has declined by between 25 and 50 percent. Actual attendance could be significantly lower, researchers note, because survey respondents tend to overreport involvement in the life of the church. Consistent with what we repeatedly hear, mainline denominations have suffered the greatest declines during this time.[1] Perhaps even more ominous are the results of polls that reveal our attitude toward the body of believers. Almost 80 percent of Americans who believe in God assert that participation in a church community is not a necessary part of their faith.[2]

But for most of us the truly moving evidence is anecdotal, gleaned from contact with individual Christians and through long-term observation of the church. I see at least three categories of believers whose perception of Christian community is a major, though often neglected, problem in the contemporary church. The first, like the 80 percent mentioned above, have an incredible ignorance about the place of Christian community in the life of a disciple. Sadly, they often practice their faith in complete isolation from other believers. The second group differs from the first mainly in its members' attitude toward corporate worship. They do attend services regularly, but they do so with minimal or no expectations about Christian community. These are the Christians who quietly slip out of church immediately after worship. They usually don't know the people sitting next to them in the pew, and they have no contact with fellow church members the other six days of the week.

11

Somehow the message they hear preached on Sunday morning fails to communicate (or persuade) that relationships with fellow Christians are a vital part of their faith journey.

Members of the third of these groups are perhaps the most filled with pathos: they are those Christians who have some idea about the church's communal potential, but who are invariably disappointed with the community they experience. Some come desperately seeking friendship and support, but find only superficial relationships. They often become church hoppers, trying to discover a church that resembles some idealized community from their past. Other Christians persevere in churches filled with conflict. Some of their community needs are met through long-term and carefully nurtured relationships in the church, but they agonize over the lack of unity in the larger congregation. Attending church is an exercise in diplomacy; words must be carefully weighed and certain issues kept off-limits to avoid opening old and recent wounds. Far from being a place where healthy Christian relationships abound and believers use God's gifts to support one another, the church becomes the primary locus of tension and divisiveness in attenders' lives.

I am convinced that we are experiencing a crisis of community in mainstream denominations. "Christians without community" has become the hallmark of the contemporary church. Whether people are ignorant of the value of Christian community or seek community but find only a pale shadow of what this fellowship might be, the effect is the same: the church does not function as it should. Dysfunctional community poisons every aspect of church life. Community is a vital issue for the church because we define and evaluate the church primarily in terms of our communal experiences. Members often told me, their pastor, of old community grievances that continued to color their attitude toward the church: no one had visited them when they were in the hospital, someone in the church had slighted them or their family, or they did not feel loved by the community. I can think of instances when individuals have left a church because they disagreed with its theology, ethics, or polity, but those instances have not been common. For most of us, the first substantive thing that "church" brings to mind is the community we experience, the quality of relationships we have with our fellow Christians. And this test of the church's integrity too often reveals a great weakness.

A good part of my motivation for writing this book comes from my own varied experiences with Christian community, enough of them negative to convince me that a significant problem exists and enough of them positive to give me a glimpse of what community might be. My most formative experience in Christian community came during the last year of my mother's long illness. My father was the primary caregiver.

He tended to my mother, cooked, cleaned, and monitored medication. It was a heavy and wearing task. As is so typical of people who grow up in small town and rural America, we children had pursued education and careers that led us far away from our first home, and we could provide little help in caring for our mother. But it was amazing the way my parents' church stepped in to help, to cook and clean, to socialize, to provide the kind of support my parents needed during the months before my mother's death. Although I had grown up in that Christian community and knew of its gracious love, the realization that others would treat my parents as their own came as a revelation.[3] It is hard to imagine how my parents would have dealt with this ordeal alone, as so many people are forced to do. In their most difficult time the Christian community made unbearable tasks bearable and through gracious acts of service reminded all of us of God's unwavering love.

Unfortunately, there is a strong pessimism in the mainstream church, even among its leaders, about the possibility of experiencing or "building" this kind of community. Pastors regularly commiserate with one another about their communal battle scars, and seminary students no longer idealize the church life that awaits them. This absence of naïveté among future pastors is perhaps most powerfully illustrated by seminary students' reaction to an illustration I sometimes employ in class. I describe for my students two communities. One, I tell them, is attractive; the other, pathetic. In the attractive one people are drawn to one another and gather often. Joy is commonly expressed and laughter is frequent. Conversation flows easily and everyone seems to be included. People willingly give of their time and money to maintain the communal environment. Problems of life fade in this place of sharing and caring. Here there is no pretense about dressing up; it's always "come as you are." The doors of the building where this community meets are almost always open. When people gather here, life seems very good indeed.

The pathetic community, I tell my students, offers an environment that is cold and sterile. People rarely gather here, at most only for a short time each week, and often grudgingly at that. When they come, they are not very friendly. One sees a few half-hearted smiles, but there is little real sharing, and it takes a long time to build relationships. There is a rather formal dress code. Tensions between various groups occur often, and conversation is stilted. The money given to maintain this community's meeting place is barely enough to cover the essentials. The building usually stands empty. Little joy is expressed here. Rather than easing life's tensions, coming together in this community seems to emphasize them.

After completing this brief description, I pose a question you have probably anticipated. One of these communities, I tell my students, is the local VFW hall; the other is the local church. Which is which? Of course they immediately realize that this exercise has been tongue-in-cheek and that my descriptions are caricatures. Still, their response is telling; invariably they indicate that the attractive community is *not* the church. And there is no great protest that Christian community is being described as such a joyless, sterile thing. Further discussion reveals that while most of these middle-aged, second-career seminary students have had positive experiences of Christian community, they have also had more than a taste of community's dark side. They will enter positions of leadership in the church with the perception that Christian community is a problem, an ideal not often realized. These future ecclesiastical leaders are quite willing to agree that it may be easier to find community in the workplace or in a club or organization than in the church.

Declining Social Capital

Certainly there is no small irony in my students' assumption about civic community. It is widely believed that American society itself has experienced a breakdown of community in the last forty years, one that has been a key factor in the communal meltdown of the church. Many Americans live in a world where there is significantly less opportunity or desire for relationships than there was in the world their grandparents inhabited. In his book *Bowling Alone: The Collapse and Revival of American Community*, Robert D. Putnam gives several reasons for the decline in "social capital" in the United States. Relatively minor, but not insignificant, is the way our involvement in civic community has been eroded because of "pressures of time and money" that result in part from the dramatic increase in two-career families. Suburbanization and the isolation borne of long commutes to work and neighborhoods with autonomous families have had a similar impact. More significant, according to Putnam, has been the effect of electronic entertainment, and especially television, of "privatizing our leisure time." Above all, Putnam points to "generational change," the evolution from the civic-minded World War II generation to subsequent generations that have never been confronted with the value and price of American community.[4]

Although people will continue to debate its causes, this breakdown of civic community is a reality we must face, especially as we cope with parallel community issues in the church. Perhaps the ideology behind this community malaise is best described by three "isms" that have come into common parlance: individualism, materialism, and postmodernism. Individualism has long been a part of the American mind, including that of the American church, but our current expression of it lies at the heart of the problem. The desire to shape and take responsibility for one's life can be a good thing, but increasingly individualism has come to mean the impulse toward autonomy, a fixation on personal needs and pleasures without concern for others.[5] This attitude is energized by materialism, here defined broadly as the desire to have all that is considered part of the American good life: leisure, entertainment, the latest electronic devices, and traditional material trappings such as a home and a car. When materialism feeds autonomy by encouraging self-centered goals and by creating a world that replaces people with things, it becomes a central issue in our loss of community. Postmodernism also plays into the hands of individualism by questioning traditional explanations of what is valuable in a society. The long-held ideal of neighborliness in American culture, for instance, may no longer be assumed by a generation wary of traditional or universal truth. For postmodernists, meaning is contextual and therefore determined individually. This is a radical departure from the more communal attitudes toward truth that prevailed earlier in the twentieth century.[6]

Perhaps the most widely read documentation of the weakening of American communities appears in Robert Bellah et al's *Habits of the Heart: Individualism and Commitment in American Life*. Through interviews with hundreds of middle-class Americans, Bellah and his group of sociologists were able to document our society's uneasy move away from community and toward the pursuit of individual happiness. Among the many graphic examples of individualism gone to seed, perhaps none is more memorable than Bellah's description of a certain Sheila, a young nurse who has gone so far as to name a religion after herself ("Sheilaism"). She identifies her own voice as the voice of God, and the core of her theology is a gentle and loving attitude toward herself.[7] Although this woman's understanding of religion may seem odd or even sick, hers is only an honest naming of the self-centered "faith" Bellah shows is common in American society.

But there are also strong indications that Americans do not feel comfortable with the breakdown of community. Many of those whom Bellah and his associates interviewed believed that the circumstances of their lives were wrenching them away from the authentic relationships their parents and grandparents experienced. There is a "profound yearning for the idealized small town" that would bring "meaning and coherence" to the lives of these middle-class Americans.[8]

A recent study by Princeton researcher Robert Wuthnow points to a similar longing. Wuthnow shows that an amazing 40 percent of Americans belong to a support group of one sort or another—a self-help group, recovery group, prayer fellowship, twelve-step gathering, or some other group. These small groups appear to be replacing more traditional forms of community. Wuthnow makes it clear, however, that participation in these small groups does not necessarily represent a flight from individualism. Individuals usually join these groups because they offer help in coping with a crisis or new situation, not because there is a desire to form long-term relationships. Support groups are successful, explains Wuthnow, because they "provide us with small, portable sources of interpersonal support."[9] Yet the popularity of small groups does indicate a felt need for the "other" in our lives, a wistfulness about traditional forms of community:

> Most people, however, seem to believe at some level that this self-centered individualism is no way to live. They may not have the security of a tight-knit neighborhood, but they want it. They may not enjoy the comfort of a warm family, but they wish they could. They value their individual freedom, but go through life feeling lonely. They desire intimacy and wonder how to find it. They cling to the conviction that they have close friends who care about them but they frequently feel distant from these friends. They worry what would happen if they were truly in need. Wanting community, and not being able to find it, they turn to other solutions, some of which become their worst enemies.[10]

How does this decline of American social capital relate to the community issues facing the church? I am convinced that we need to take the causes of the breakdown of civic community very seriously, because they will certainly appear within the walls of the church as well. Christian community must know how to respond to an individualism energized by materialism and postmodernism. In a sense, society is the schoolhouse even for those who seek Christian community, but it is difficult for someone who has never experienced communal life outside the church to suddenly comprehend the issues in a church community that is based upon loving relationships. But we as Christians need to beware lest we become so overwhelmed by the world's challenges to community that we assume Christian community is an impossible goal. Christian community is not a carbon copy of secular communities, even when they are at their best. It is, as we shall see, far more radical and far more dependent upon an outside source of empowerment.

The lack of community in American society does not preclude Christian community any more than a robust secular community would guarantee it. Suddenly turning history back to the 1940s or 1950s, when people apparently did find community in their small-town or urban neighborhoods, would not ensure the miraculous appearance in our churches of the kind of community I see described in Paul's letters. The breakdown of community in our culture is not an insurmountable barrier to Christian community. In fact, it might even be seen as an opportunity. Thousands of people in our society are lonely and tired of their self-centered pursuits; they long for the kind of community the church can offer. This yearning for authentic relationships might lead people to a community that has its foundation in God's love.

Paul and Christian Community

Before we begin an interpretation of 1 Corinthians to see how Paul responds to specific community issues, it is important that we have an overview of the apostle's understanding of Christian community. I have always felt that *community* is a difficult word to define not only because we invariably belong to several different communities but also because we use the word in two distinct ways. When I ask people to tell me about their community, they most commonly respond by talking about their civic community or neighborhood. Employed in this way, *community* refers to a group of people who have something in common; they live in a certain area, are represented by the same elected officials, use the same stores and schools, and walk the same streets. The word is defined quite differently, however, when I ask people where they experience or find community. When I ask in this way, people respond by speaking about face-to-face relationships with others, bonds of friendship or neighborliness that enrich their lives. Of course a single group of people can be defined both by what they have in common and by how they relate. A good example of this kind of community is an Alcoholics Anonymous group. What the participants have in common is obvious; they share an addiction to alcohol and a desire to be free from that addiction. The nature of their relationships is equally important; here people find the support and friendship they need to challenge their substance abuse.

Although sociologists categorize communities in various ways: according to size, level of intimacy, type of organization, whether membership is voluntary, the relationship between members and the world, the task or goal of the community, and so on. I, on the other hand, keep coming back to my two questions, which are among the most essential, especially in terms of initial definition: "What do the members of a group have in common?" and "What kind of relationships do they have with one another?" Put more simply and personally, we need to ask *what* we share with the members of our group and *how* we share it. These questions are necessary as we attempt to understand the nature of Christian community, and especially its Pauline definition.

Paul uses a certain word for "sharing" or "having something in common" far more than any other New Testament writer. The noun form of the word *koinōnia* is one of those few Greek words, along with *agapē* (love) and *metanoia* (repentance), that is regularly used in the church. Countless youth groups and adult study classes have come to understand *koinōnia* primarily as a relational term meaning "fellowship among believers," especially on the basis of its use in Acts 2:42. This is certainly a legitimate translation, and Paul also uses the word in this way. Several times the apostle employs forms of *koinōnia* to describe the sharing of material blessings that grows out of Christian love: "Through the testing of this ministry you glorify God by your obedience to the confession of the gospel of Christ and by the generosity of your sharing (*tēs koinōnias*) with them and with all others" (2 Corinthians 9:13; cf. 2 Corinthians 8:4; Romans 15:26; Galatians 6:6). And in Galatians 2:9 Paul uses *koinōnia* to speak of the love relationship that exists among Christians: during his visit to Jerusalem, the so-called pillars of the church gave to Paul and Barnabas "the right hand of fellowship" (*koinōnia*).[11]

But it may come as a surprise to those who have come to understand *koinōnia* in terms of *how* we share that in Paul the word functions primarily to describe *what* we share. The divisions at Corinth are challenged already in the thanksgiving of the letter, when Paul reminds his hearers what they have in common in Jesus Christ: "God is faithful; by him you were called into the fellowship (*koinōnia*) of his Son, Jesus Christ our Lord" (1 Corinthians 1:9). Similar is 1 Corinthians 10:16, where Paul asks whether their partaking of the cup and bread is not a sharing (*koinōnia*) in the body and blood of Christ. In 2 Corinthians 1:7, Paul speaks of the common experience (*koinōnos*) of Christian suffering (cf. Philippians 3:10). To the Philippians, another community apparently experiencing some discord, Paul issues encouragement by affirming their "sharing (*koinōnia*) in the Spirit" (2:1), using words very similar to those found in the thanksgiving: "I thank my God . . . because of your sharing (*koinōnia*) in the gospel from the first day until now" (1:3–5), "for all of you share (*syngkoinōnos*) in God's grace with me" (1:7).

Recognizing this function of *koinōnia* is important because it mirrors Paul's understanding of community throughout his letters. Paul is not simply concerned with the nature of relationships between Christians, but also with the source and empowerment of these relationships in Jesus Christ. It is impossible to understand how Christians share without also understanding what they share, and both the *how* and the *what* of this commonality are radically different from what we see in society's definition of community.

What We Share

Like a family that cannot be understood apart from its traditions, beliefs, and even dark secrets, the community that Paul describes is one in which members have a shared reality that precedes and explains the relationships they have with one another. Over and over in his letters, Paul emphasizes that one of the most basic bonds in Christian community is the realization that we cannot be right before God on the basis of our own attempts at righteousness. Paul reminds his readers what they were like "before": enslaved to the elemental spirits (Galatians 4:8–9), followers of idols (1 Thessalonians 1:9), and practicing every sin imaginable (1 Corinthians 6:9–11). In the first three chapters of Romans, Paul talks about the dilemma of both Jews and Gentiles. Gentiles fall short because they fail to follow the God they see revealed in nature (Romans 1:18–23). Jews are unable to keep the law God has revealed to them (Romans 2:17–24). Quoting Psalm 14, Paul concludes that "there is no one who is righteous, not even one" (Romans 3:10).

Paul is especially concerned about the human situation in relationship to God's law, because he has been constantly challenged by Jewish Christians who assert that Gentile Christians must keep the law (see Galatians and Philippians 3). Although Paul does recognize the value of the law (Galatians 3:19–24), his main concern is the law's ineffectiveness in the face of human sin. In one especially pathos-filled passage, Paul uses the rhetorical "I" to illustrate not only that humans cannot do what the law prescribes ("I can will what is right, but I cannot do it") but also how the law apparently lures us to do evil ("I would not have known what it is to covet if the law had not said, 'You shall not covet'" [Romans 7:7–25]).

Even more treacherous, perhaps, is how people attempt to keep the law of works, only to exhibit an attitude of boastfulness (Romans 3:27) or self-righteousness before God (Romans 9:30–10:4). Paul makes it clear that even our pious strivings can be a problem. As Robin Scroggs puts it, Paul portrays sinners as both "helpless and hostile,"[12] helpless in the sense that we are unable to achieve righteousness on our own, and hostile in that our attempts to keep the law are often declarations of independence from God as an overbearing father. At one point in Philippians Paul lists his credentials and achievements only to assert that they are all rubbish (*skybalon*, a word that should actually be translated more strongly, as "excrement") in comparison to what God has done for him in Jesus Christ (3:8).

Paul does not use his numerous references to this sinful predicament to harangue his hearers to repentance as some fly-by-night evangelist might. His primary concern is to emphasize what believers have already left behind and, of course, to encourage them to continue in the faith. In terms of community, Paul is making an essential statement: sin and our inability to achieve righteousness link us together. They are the great equalizers. We are all heirs of Adam and his sin (Romans 5:12–21; 1 Corinthians 15:21–22, 45–49). None of us, no matter what our personal or religious achievements, has any claim before God.

Of course Christians share far more than their recognition that they are unable to save themselves. Above all, Paul's letters show that we are linked in the salvation that God offers in Christ. The barriers that separated us from God have been removed, and a new relationship has been established. Community has its origin in an act of God. Paul uses various word pictures to describe Christ's saving activity. At times he talks about Christians being "in Christ" or "in the Spirit" and about how they thus participate in the new life and empowerment of Christ (Romans 6:1–11; 8:1–11). At other times he focuses on how Christ's death on the cross deals with the problem of sin. Often he simply states that Christ died for us and for our sins (1 Corinthians 15:3; 2 Corinthians 5:15; 1 Thessalonians 5:10). In Romans 3:25 he speaks of Christ as a blood atonement, much like a Jew would have spoken of the temple sacrifice of a lamb or dove. Paul's favorite word to depict Christ's saving activity is "justification," a term that conjures up a courtroom setting (Romans 3:24; 5:9; Galatians 2:16). In Jesus Christ we have God's acquittal, and no one can ever bring any charge against us (Romans 8:31). Even more, we are reconciled to God (Romans 5:10–11), experiencing the fullness of God's love (1 Corinthians 13:12–13; 2 Corinthians 8:1–2).

The apostle never tires of telling his readers that this salvation in Christ is a free gift, an act of grace (Romans 3:24). People receive this salvation by "faith," a word that Paul uses to describe both a humble openness to salvation and an attitude of trust and obedience. Individuals must have this faith, as did Abraham, a favorite example of Paul's (Romans 4; Galatians 3). But one of Paul's primary concerns is how Christian community functions in light of its *common* faith. Christian community is, first and foremost, a corporate experience of God's grace. What we share has its source in God and is transformative, a movement from death to life. Paul envisions a people bound together by a near-death experience of a religious sort. They know what it was like to be enemies of God, and now they know what it means to have a relationship with God, a love relationship that brings peace (Romans 5:1) and a new status as God's children (Galatians 3:23–4:7).

Another way of thinking about this drama of sin and salvation that binds Christians together is to consider the temporal paradox that is always present in Paul's description of life in Christ. Like that of many Jews of his day, Paul's theology can be termed "apocalyptic eschatology."[13] It is eschatological because he believes that God's actions in Jesus Christ represent the final act in salvation history (*eschaton* means "last thing"). It is apocalyptic because he believes that "this age" (1 Corinthians 1:20; 2:6–8) is so corrupt and sinful it must be replaced by a new age, one that is initiated by a sudden appearance of God's Messiah, at a time when all powers submit to God and his rule is complete (1 Corinthians 15:24–25; *apokalypsis* refers to a revelation about how and when this age will end).

But in terms of *when* the new age arrives, Paul's eschatological vision is unique, even radical, compared to that of contemporary Jewish thinkers: in Jesus Christ, God's future has already entered our world. The Messiah has come, and those who trust in him have already been changed. They have been redeemed and justified, reconciled to God. Believers are new creations (2 Corinthians 5:17). The hallmark of the new age, the resurrection, has already occurred in Christ, and his followers have been raised to new life as well (Romans 6:1–11). Christians, Paul tells us, are transformed people who must not conform themselves to the present age (Romans 12:2).

Yet as wonderful as this message is, the imperative in Romans 12:2 hints at the tension the message creates. Why do transformed people need to be commanded to avoid conforming to this age? And why does this age with its temptations continue to exist even after the Messiah has arrived? Anyone can tell that if the new has arrived, it has done so in the midst of the old. According to Paul, this tension is one of the most significant things Christians share with one another. If "angst" is perhaps too negative a way of describing our reaction to being redeemed people in an unredeemed world, then certainly "the experience of temporal dissonance" is not. We share with other Christians the dilemma of striving to be in actuality what God says we already are in Jesus Christ. Paul's gospel reminds us that believers share the conviction that God works not only in the present and with individuals but also in the broad sweep of history and on a corporate level—see what he says about God's plan for Jews and Gentiles in Romans 9–11. And because God controls history and moves it in unexpected ways, we share with those in our Christian communities the perception that we live in a kind of time warp; together we see the present with wary and critical eyes because we have been given a glimpse of God's future.

Those who have experienced the inbreaking of the new age are bound together by a desire to please God for what he has done for them in Jesus Christ. Certainly the best example of the community's response to God for this salvation is corporate worship, and Paul is very protective of it (1 Corinthians 11:17–34; 14:1–40). In fact, Paul sees all of life as a worshiplike response to God (Romans 12:1–2). Much of this response has to do with how Christians relate to one another, a topic we will discuss in the next section. But Christians share many other things because of their salvation in Christ. Paul often tells his hearers that they may experience hostility or persecution because of their faith (2 Corinthians 4:7–12; 1 Thessalonians 2:14; Philippians 1:29). Christians share the necessity of making ethical decisions on the basis of their new relationship with God (Romans 12:14–21). They share the task of learning how to relate to the world as people who have been transformed (Romans 13; 1 Corinthians 5:1–6:20). And Christians share not only their present relationship with God but also the assurance that it will lead to eternal life and the resurrection of the body (1 Corinthians 15; 2 Corinthians 5:1–10; 1 Thessalonians 4:13–18). We long for a time when the tension between present and future will disappear.

Together as Christians we recognize what God has done for us and respond in a worship that permeates all of life. In short, what we share as community is our new relationship with God, a relationship that so shapes our reality that it forever changes who we are. It is this love relationship with God that determines what our relationship with our fellow community members will be, or how we share with one another.

How We Share

Paul believes that the salvation God offers in Jesus Christ signals the arrival of the messianic age. The reign of God that Israel had anticipated over the centuries, a time when justice would prevail and God would show his love to all people, has become a reality in Christ. Nowhere is this stated more powerfully than in 2 Corinthians.

> So if anyone is in Christ, there is a new creation: everything old has passed away; see, everything has become new! All this is from God, who reconciled us to himself through Christ, and has given us the ministry of reconciliation. . . . So we are ambassadors for Christ, since God is making his appeal through us. . . . See, now is the acceptable time; see, now is the day of salvation! (5:17–18, 20; 6:2)

Paul describes the old age as one of restrictions, even slavery. The law imprisoned us and guarded us (Galatians 3:23); we were slaves of sin (Romans 6:15–23). We were children of a slave woman, but in Jesus Christ we have become children of Sarah, the free woman (Galatians 4:21–31). Entrance into the new age means we have been freed from our slavery to sin and freed to serve God. Just as important, we are now free to love one another in the way God intended. As Paul says in Galatians 5:13–14:

For you were called to freedom, brothers and sisters; only do not use your freedom as an opportunity for self-indulgence, but through love become slaves to one another. For the whole law is summed up in a single commandment, "You shall love your neighbor as yourself."

The love that lies at the center of Christian relationships is both defined and modeled in Jesus Christ. In Philippians, Paul encourages his readers to humble themselves before one another (2:3) and to follow the example of Christ who "did not regard equality with God as something to be exploited, but emptied himself, taking the form of slave" (2:6–7). Christians are those who "have been taught by God to love one another" (1 Thessalonians 4:9). No clearer definition of the love operating in community can be found than that in 1 Corinthians 13:4–7:

Love is patient; love is kind; love is not envious or boastful or arrogant or rude. It does not insist on its own way; it is not irritable or resentful; it does not rejoice in wrongdoing, but rejoices in the truth. It bears all things, believes all things, hopes all things, endures all things.

Christians become ambassadors of the new age inaugurated by Christ when they practice this love in community. Paul's letters are full of advice about how such love should affect our conduct toward one another in daily situations. On the basis of the presence of this love, Paul can assume that Gentile Christians will contribute to a collection for the poor in Jerusalem (2 Corinthians 8–9). He expects Christians to relinquish their newfound freedom out of love for one another (1 Corinthians 8; Romans 14). Love allows the Corinthians to forgive a community member who has gone astray (2 Corinthians 2:5–10), and it is the essential reason for using church discipline (1 Corinthians 5). Love motivates the Thessalonians to treat their community members honorably, as brothers and sisters in Christ (1 Thessalonians 4:1–12). Paul reminds the Philippians to experience the joy that grows out of their communal love (Philippians 4:4–7, 10–14).

Christ's love practiced in community signals the coming of the new age in that it radically redefines *whom* one may love. Paul believes that divisions caused by the law lie at the heart of the social stratification he sees in his world. Law is used to restrict membership in a community; it defines who is in and who is out (clean versus unclean, Jew versus Gentile, man versus woman). With the coming of Christ, old barriers erected by the law, our disciplinarian (Galatians 3:24–25), are no longer in effect. As Paul says in Galatians 3:28: "There is no longer Jew or Greek, there is no longer slave or free, there is no longer male and female; for all of you are one in Christ Jesus." Christians love one another with a love that is blind to the distinctions so common in society.

The Holy Spirit helps Christians to practice love toward one another. The link between the Holy Spirit and community is perhaps best seen in Paul's discussion of spiritual gifts. Paul makes it clear that God empowers us through the Spirit with gifts that are to be used not for individual purposes, but for the "common good" (1 Corinthian 12:7). Gifts such as wisdom, faith, healing, miracles, prophecy, the discernment of spirits, and speaking in and interpreting tongues (1 Corinthians 12:8–10) are properly used for building up the community (1 Corinthians 14:3–5, 12, 26). Not only does God expect Christians to have relationships with one another that are based on the love we know in Christ, but he also empowers these relationships. God's ongoing presence through the Spirit and the Spirit's relationship-sustaining gifts account for Paul's minimal concern for church administration. The church functions not because it has well-defined offices, but because members are attuned to the Spirit's revelations (1 Corinthians 2:11; 12:27–30) and lovingly use their gifts for the larger body.

On the basis of Paul's understanding of what and how we share, a Christian community can be defined as a group of Christians whose expression of love for one another is modeled on and made possible by God's great act of love in Jesus Christ. Defined in this way, *Christian community* may sound like a synonym for *church*, and at times it is difficult to avoid using the terms interchangeably. But there is a difference. *Church*, at least when it is defined more formally, denotes a broader institution that performs several functions, of which nurturing the relationships that lie at the core of community is only one.

In his classic *Models of the Church*, Avery Dulles uses five models to speak of the traditional task of the church. The church as *institution* concerns itself with governance and organization. The church as *sacrament*, as one might guess, administers the sacraments and protects their purity. The church as *herald* proclaims the Christian message. As *servant*, the church ministers to the various needs of the world. Finally, Dulles uses the term *mystical communion* to refer to what I have labeled Christian community. Obviously there is considerable overlap between these categories, especially when it comes to our primary concern, community. The love relationship that binds us together as Christians will certainly influence all our other ecclesiastical tasks; in fact, it could easily be argued that community is the most foundational of these five models of the church.[14]

Simply put, *Christian community* describes how we live together as members of a church, the love and fellowship we experience with one another because of our common bond in Jesus Christ. Without denying the many ways in which Christian community is often less than it might be, it is absolutely vital to understand how the community we experience in our congregations distinguishes itself from the community we experience in the other social groups we inhabit. Both what we share and how we share in the church are radically different from what and how we share in the world. Christian community is not simply about sharing the same zip code and being neighborly to those around us, as important as these things might be. Christian community is unique because it grows out of the transforming love of Jesus Christ and therefore allows us to love one another in sacrificial and inclusive ways.

Although one might hope that Christians would be part of a broad range of civic organizations, Christian community is not optional, like a club that one may or may not join. It lies at the center of who we are as disciples. And our definition of Christian community also means that we must beware of thinking we can build community as we might in clubs and organizations. Christian community is not simply a matter of having more potluck dinners or softball games. The love that we have for one another is inexorably linked to the love we have known in Christ. Without discipleship there can be no fellowship.

Barriers to Community in the Corinthian Church

For contemporary Christians anxious to hear what Scripture has to say about community, there is no better New Testament book with which to begin than 1 Corinthians. No other book is so completely devoted to the topic of Christian community, and no other book rivals 1 Corinthians in applicability to our current situation. And the striking relevance of the issues addressed in 1 Corinthians is further enhanced because Paul invariably discusses the specific problems or barriers to community as well as his suggested solutions. First Corinthians is not an abstract discussion of the theology of community, but perhaps the finest example of Pauline contextual thought, a product of the mature pastoral theologian at work.

Paul systematically moves from one community barrier to the next, not only showing how dangerous the Corinthians' communal divisions are but also explaining how the Corinthians can be unified in mind and purpose in Jesus Christ (1:10). The Corinthians are divided because of an improper attitude toward Christian leaders (chapters 1–4). Their unity is threatened by immorality (chapters 5–6), gender issues (chapter 7; 11:2–16), a skewed understanding of Christian freedom (chapters 8–10), and class divisions (11:17–34). They are split over their use of spiritual gifts (chapters 12–14), and some of them even doubt whether believers are raised from the dead (chapter 15). At every turn Paul addresses another barrier to community that seems to threaten the life of the Corinthian church. Some of these have come to his attention through a recent letter from Corinth (7:1; 8:1; 12:1); others have arrived by way of Paul's ecclesiastical grapevine (1:11; 5:1; 15:12). This picture of the early church is quite different from what we see in Acts. An ironic sort of encouragement comes in knowing that the community issues confronting us are no worse than those facing Paul in that incredibly confused first-century congregation.

I will present relevant historical information as I discuss each chapter of 1 Corinthians (and see the chapter introductions that appear in most commentaries), but here I offer an overview. Corinth was a typical first-century southern European trade city. It lay at the center of important Greek water and land trade routes. The various religions and philosophies of both East and West were well represented. Corinth had been destroyed by the Romans in 146 B.C.E.; it was rebuilt by Julius Caesar in 44 B.C.E. Strabo, a first-century C.E. historian, states that the city was populated especially by former slaves. Their entrepreneurial spirit and the city's excellent location gave Corinth a reputation for being a thriving commercial center. Paul founded the church at Corinth between C.E. 50 and 52 and wrote 1 Corinthians from Ephesus about two years later (16:8; see Luke's account of Paul's time in Corinth in Acts 18:1–17). First Corinthians is actually the second in a series of letters written to the church (5:9); Paul's amazing record of correspondence shows just how tense the relationship between the apostle and this new congregation was at times (see 2 Corinthians 10–13).[15]

Considering the number and variety of barriers to community facing the Corinthians, is it possible to give a comprehensive explanation for their communal woes, to define the Corinthians' problem? As you might guess, biblical scholars have long wrestled with this issue, and their explanations vary widely. In the 1950s and 1960s it was common to interpret the Corinthian situation as a product of early Gnostic thought. Scholars such as Walter Schmithals (*Gnosticism in Corinth: An Investigation of the Letters to the Corinthians*) and Hans Conzelmann (*1 Corinthians*) believed they saw in the Corinthian church the same christological and ethical leanings that characterized second-century Christian Gnosticism.[16] The Corinthians were infatuated with esoteric knowledge and wisdom (chapters 1–4); they sought out mystical or pneumatic experiences (chapter 14) and practiced an ethic that denied the importance of the body (chapters 5–7 and 15). But while many of the issues raised by these scholars continue to attract attention, their Gnostic solution has weaknesses. There appears to be no unifying Gnostic mythology at Corinth, and Paul does not address the Corinthians as if they possessed a well-defined alternative Christology. Many of the issues identified above can be explained simply as a product of the Corinthians' Greco-Roman religious and cultural context.

A more helpful approach comes to us through scholars, such as Gerd Theissen (*The Social Setting of Pauline Christianity: Essays on Corinth*) and later Dale Martin (*The Corinthian Body*), who employ a social analysis of the Corinthian community.[17] According to these scholars, class conflict played a central role in the tensions at Corinth. The social stratification characteristic of the Hellenistic world was present in the Corinthian church as well: the rich failed to share with the poor during the Lord's Supper (11:17–34); the rich more readily used lawyers (6:1–11) and ate of the meat sacrificed to idols (chapter 8–10). Perhaps, as Martin argues, the class differences in the Corinthian church are also the origin of the tensions concerning the human body (chapters 5, 7, 15).

Although her method is more literary than sociological, Antoinette Wire's *The Corinthian Women Prophets: A Reconstruction through Paul's Rhetoric* also focuses on social conflict, specifically tensions between the genders. According to Wire, inclusion in the church affected the social standing of first-century women and men differently. Paul, writing from the point of view of an educated male, asserts that entrance into the faith involves a relinquishing of status on the basis of the foolishness of the cross (1:18–31; chapter 9). But to women and lower-class Corinthians, the Christian faith would have meant liberation from old social norms (chapter 7; 11:2–16), empowerment (chapter 14), and wisdom (1:18–31). Thus Paul and higher-class Corinthians stand at odds with a group of freewheeling women prophets. Wire believes that one of Paul's main reasons for writing the letter is to silence these women (14:34–35) and convince lower-class Christians to remain as they are (7:17–24).[18]

These probing analyses of the social setting of the Corinthian church have taught us a great deal about the causes for communal unrest there, and they will certainly inform future studies. But they too have their shortcomings. These scholars tend to see their particular social issues everywhere in 1 Corinthians, even in places where the application seems strained. I would suggest a more modest approach to use when trying to explain the strife in the Corinthian church, one that takes these historical and social studies very seriously, but that, like the earlier proponents of the Gnoticism perspective, tries to understand the theological motivations in the community as well. Each of the community problems Paul needed to address grew out of the Corinthians' inability to let the gospel message fully reshape their gentile, Greco-Roman lives, whether because they misunderstood that message or because they rejected it outright. They were Hellenists through and through, and this eschatological, cross-centered, body-affirming Jewish sect called Christianity demanded that they enter another theological and ethical world. It is no surprise that these residents of Corinth would seek rhetorical wisdom, be unconcerned with immorality and the preservation of the body, be infatuated with asceticism and spiritual empowerment, and preserve distinctions between rich and poor. The Corinthians were simply trying to be Christians with a minimal amount of social and theological disturbance. Does that sound familiar?

Although the Corinthians could perhaps at times plead ignorance (see 1 Corinthians 15 and the issue of the resurrection of the body), most often they appear to have either intentionally rejected (11:17–34) or radicalized (chapter 5, 11:2–16) Paul's teaching. Paul is right to call them arrogant or puffed up, as he does especially at the beginning of the letter (4:6–7; 5:2, 6). Sin, as it manifests itself in the Hellenistic world, can legitimately be considered the community problem at Corinth. Hopefully this assessment will not tempt us to dissociate ourselves from the Corinthians, but will help us realize how deep our bond with them is. Not only were the specific communal problems at Corinth very much like the ones we face, but even their rebellious attitude is more than faintly familiar.

In his poem "The Entrance of Sin," Scott Cairns gives a powerful reinterpretation of the biblical account of the origin of sin. Long before the eating of the illicit fruit and human disobedience before God, sin entered the world when during an evening walk through the garden the man rejected the woman's's offer to hold his hand. In the beginning, according to Cairn's poem, sin was not so much a rebellion against God as it was an almost inexplicable desire for autonomy from others. In spite of all the recognizable good that our relationships bring, we are somehow tempted to separate ourselves from others. This act of differentiation reflects an assumed superiority that, when we think about it, is not at all unlike the attitude that prompted Adam and Eve to eat of the tree of the knowledge of good and evil (Genesis 3:6). Sin is the pursuit of the self-centered exhilaration we feel when we reject relationships and therefore community. As Cairns puts it, sin entered the world when Adam and Eve failed to curtail this "developing habit of resistance," when the paradoxical desire for separation from the beauty of relationships became "irresistible."[19]

We can predict what form the rejection of Christian community will take by looking at the world in which a believer resides. Our sins against community reflect American society, just as the Corinthians' reflected theirs. But what we share most essentially with the Corinthians, indeed with all of humanity, is the impulse to separate ourselves from others. It lies deep within us and is one of the most basic struggles we face. We also share with the Corinthians the good news that in Jesus Christ we are new creations; this is the impetus to be what we already are in God's eyes. Yet we know that as long as we are in this age we will face barriers to community. Loving one another as Christ loves us, God's vision for humanity, will continue to be put in the imperative mood. Paul's letter to the Corinthians is an essential guide for the contemporary church because it forces us to come to terms with both the importance of community and our resistance to it.

Community
and Christian Leaders

1 Corinthians 1–4

There is always a link between Christology and discipleship, between what we believe about Christ and how we live. Ideally, the Christ of our faith shapes our walk as Christians, but the opposite can occur as well: sometimes we live in a certain way and then "create" a Christ to suit our needs. Paul's words to the Corinthians in 1 Corinthians 1–4 have always reminded me of the three passion predictions in the Gospel of Mark (8:27–9:1; 9:30–37; 10:32–45), because in both places we see that our lives as disciples are never theologically innocent. In Mark, the disciples' desire for status and power makes it impossible for them to understand that Christ's mission will be fulfilled in the cross. At Corinth, church members squabble over rhetorical wisdom in a way that reflects their inability to see "Christ crucified" (1 Corinthians 1:23). For both the Corinthians and the disciples in Mark, an easy acceptance of the world's standards skews their Christology.

Paul both begins and closes his letter with community issues that are explicitly christological. The Corinthians may not be aware of how their divisions define them christologically, but Paul's statement about the foolishness of the cross forms the center of his argument (1:18–31). Various groups at Corinth have come into tension with each other because they are infatuated with certain leaders and enamored of their preaching. Both this specific barrier to community and its theological origin are acutely relevant for the contemporary church. First Corinthians 1–4 is a marvelous case study for those of us who might be tempted to idolize our preachers without regard for how it might affect community.

1 Corinthians 1–2

Unlike Galatians, in which the heat of the moment causes Paul to omit the thanksgiving of the letter, 1 Corinthians has the typical introductory parts: a statement of sender and recipient (1:1–2), a salutation (v. 3), and a thanksgiving (vv. 4–9).[1] Although here Paul is not so upset that he abbreviates his standard form, it is easy to see by the way he telegraphs upcoming issues in the letter that the problems at Corinth are very much on his mind. Paul begins by making it clear who he is, taking a defensive posture we will see often in the letter. His authority is based on the fact that he has been called to be an apostle of Jesus Christ by God's will (v. 1; cf. Galatians 1:1).

If Paul's description of himself is an affirmation of what he now is, his description of the Corinthians can be seen as his hope for what the Corinthians might become. Or to put it in more Pauline terms, Paul is encouraging the Corinthians to be what they already are in God's eyes. It is hard to imagine that this is the same disturbed congregation he will address in the following chapters. The Corinthians are the "church of God"; they are "sanctified in Christ Jesus" and "called to be saints" (v. 2). He deftly reminds them that they are part of a larger community (v. 2), an argument he will use again (11:16). They are the recipients of God's grace (v. 4) and have been enriched in the things they so desperately crave: speech and knowledge (v. 5). They are not lacking in any spiritual gift, an affirmation with which the Corinthians would surely agree (v. 7). All of this is subtly put into context with Paul's reminder that the Corinthians are still living in a broken age and that they must persevere in the faithful life until Christ returns (v. 8). Paul concludes the thanksgiving with a statement that will echo in various ways throughout the letter: that their fellowship (*koinōnia*) in Jesus Christ is what binds them together as a community (v. 9).

Immediately after these important opening remarks, Paul records what many think is the purpose statement for the entire letter: "Now I appeal to you, brothers and sisters, by the name of our Lord Jesus Christ, that all of you be in agreement and that there be no divisions among you, but that you be united in the same mind and the same purpose" (v. 10). From the very beginning Paul lets the congregation at Corinth know that he is well aware of the divisions (*schismata*) that are splitting their church apart. Paul's statement of the problem also contains his desired solution, that they be the family they claim to be ("brothers and sisters") and that they be united in mind and purpose in their Lord Jesus Christ. Paul's opening words are a call for communal unity, an appeal we will hear again and again.

The community problem Paul confronts initially is chosen with good reason; he knows that it represents a serious theological misunderstanding, and, almost as important, he recognizes that his own authority as a leader is being challenged and that he must defend his ministry if this letter is to have any impact at all. The Corinthians have divided themselves into groups (1:12); there is quarreling (1:11; 3:3), jealousy (3:3), and immaturity (3:1–3). This community problem has its immediate origin in an illegitimate loyalty to Christian leaders. People "belong" to their leaders (1:12; 3:4) and boast in them (3:21) in a way that makes them critical of other leaders, including Paul, and hence causes splits in the church. This leadership problem has arisen because the people have an improper desire for "wisdom" (*sophia*, 1:17, 19, 21–22, 24–27, 30, and so on). People seek this wisdom in their leaders, failing to understand the implications of the cross and the true nature of Christian proclamation (1:17–25).

From "Chloe's people" (v. 11), whose report he considers reliable, Paul hears that members of the Corinthian church are quarreling and are divided into groups on the basis of their allegiance to certain leaders. The apostle even makes it sound as though they are using slogans to indicate a personal attachment to their favorite: "I belong to Paul"; "I belong to Apollos"; "I belong to Cephas"; "I belong to Christ" (v. 12). Scholars have expended a tremendous amount of energy trying to discover specifics about these groups, but more questions remain than answers. Had Peter (Cephas) actually been to Corinth, or is this group simply claiming his reputation as an acknowledged leader? Are we to take the Christ group literally, or is Paul simply speaking ironically of an exclusivist attitude? Does the fact that the Corinthian church is composed of smaller units called house churches play some role in these divisions, with each house church, perhaps, having its own esteemed and exalted leader? Certainly discussion about these issues will continue. What we can know about this situation, however, gives a fairly clear picture of the dilemma Paul is facing. We know that Apollos, who is an enthusiastic and eloquent teacher of Scripture (Acts 18:24–28), is probably a major figure in this dispute, because Paul refers to him again in chapter 3 (vv. 4–6, 22). It is also obvious that if a significant portion of the Corinthian church "belongs" to groups not led by Paul, then these people are not supporters of Paul. Paul's leadership is being challenged. People are boasting in someone other than their founding father.

On what basis are the Corinthians lining up behind their leaders, in many cases choosing someone other than Paul? Although Paul's disclaimer about his baptizing activity might seem to be a clue (1:13–17), he brings up the issue primarily to show how absurd it is to confuse their leaders with Christ. *Paul* was not crucified for them, nor were they baptized in his name! Paul's vigorous discussion of human wisdom in comparison to the "foolishness" of God in 1:17–2:5 indicates that human wisdom lies at the heart of the conflict. But in exactly what way has it become a problem in the Corinthian church? Paul's words in 1:17 are pivotal. There the apostle makes it clear that he feels compelled to defend his *preaching*. Counter to the expectations of the majority of the Corinthians, Paul does not preach with "eloquent wisdom," but in a way that intentionally acknowledges the empowerment of the cross of Christ. Paul appears to be suspicious of rhetorical wisdom, which may stand in tension with the radical message of the cross.

Until about a decade ago scholars often assumed that in 1 Corinthians (and especially in chapters 1–4) Paul is combating what can be called a "wisdom Christology." This wisdom, perhaps of Gnostic or Hellenistic-Jewish origin, stands in opposition to Paul's theology of the cross.[2] According to these scholars' view, the people of Corinth are anxious to follow leaders who see Christ as a dispenser of spiritual wisdom and empowerment, not as one who would actually come in human form, suffer, and die. In other words, it was thought that Paul is fighting a dangerous christological heresy at Corinth. The problem with this interpretation, however, is that in 1 Corinthians Paul presents no sustained argument against a wisdom Christology and gives no indication that he is battling the kind of involved mythological system found in mature Gnosticism. There are many divisive issues at Corinth, and most of them, like the one in chapters 1–4, are related to a christological misunderstanding. But it is hardly possible to link them all to Gnostic or Hellenistic-Jewish wisdom teachings, and Paul's patient and fatherly approach does not point to a pitched christological duel.

Current interpretation, rightly I think, sees the discussion in chapters 1–4 in the context of Greco-Roman rhetoric. The wisdom Paul is wary of is the wisdom of the orator, the wisdom associated with rhetorical excellence. Paul is not combating a voiced christological heresy, but an improper congregational understanding of preaching.[3] The Corinthians are attracted to their leaders on the basis of their ability to preach with wisdom, eloquence, and power. We whose educational background has given us so little experience in speech or rhetoric often fail to realize how important oratory is in the ancient Roman Empire. Advanced education, usually reserved for the elite, consists almost entirely of training in rhetoric. An accomplished speaker is skilled in the use of voice and style and understands the various methods for making speech persuasive. The polished orator can read the audience, manipulate it, and win its favor. *Wisdom* and *power* are terms that are frequently used in descriptions of the orator's art. In Paul's day people have an insatiable appetite for oratory—even three- and four-hour speeches— and the best of the orators are honored as heroes, even god-like creatures. The people of Corinth are certainly no exception in their enthusiasm for eloquence. Dio Chrysostom's *Discourses* tell about the orator Favorinus and his visits to Corinth. The population was so enamored with his eloquence that they erected a bronze statue of him in a place of high honor, the city library.[4] In a way that may be difficult for us to understand, oratory is an obsession in the Greco-Roman world, and successful orators can achieve recognition, power, and status.

Paul does not preach with eloquent wisdom, and thus his sermons do not measure up when compared with the kind of oratory many of the Corinthians desire. In 1:17–2:5 Paul is defending himself against a common perception at Corinth, that he is a less-than-adequate preacher. This perception continues to follow Paul: addressing his conflict with the so-called super-apostles in 2 Corinthians, he admits that some think he is "untrained in speech" (2 Corinthians 11:6) and that his speech is "contemptible" (10:10). Paul is in conflict with the Corinthians concerning the nature of good preaching, and especially about *how* one preaches, about the form and style of preaching. The kind of wisdom about which Paul expresses concern in 1 Corinthians is not an alternate Christology being preached in Corinth. Rather, it is the wisdom associated with fine oratory, with the kind of preaching that points to the persuasive skills of the orator.

This does not mean that the Corinthians' desire for rhetorical wisdom has no theological implications. Paul realizes that their attitude toward preaching and preachers is in tension with the message of the cross, and his first response to this problem is a highly theological one. And the attitude the Corinthians display with regard to rhetorical wisdom is a factor in other issues Paul must confront in this letter. Many in the church seem to have a high view of their own knowledge, authority, and spirituality, and it is these "wise" at Corinth who are especially critical of Paul's ministry.

Paul writes not only to defend himself as preacher and apostle, but especially to help the Corinthians gain a proper understanding of preaching, hoping to defuse the attraction to certain preachers that is splitting the church. His strategy is an interesting one. In one of the most rhetorically sophisticated passages in all of his letters (what irony!), Paul attempts to show that for the Christian preacher there is a relationship between what one preaches and how one preaches (1:18–2:5). The cross of Jesus Christ, the essential content of Christian preaching, is such an unexpected and irrational message of salvation that it can realistically be described as "foolishness" (1:18, 20–21, 25, 27). How one preaches must not stand in tension with or become an obstacle to this foolishness. The sermon must not become a monument to human eloquence that detracts from this radical foolishness or empties the cross of its power (1:17). Paul uses himself as an example: "my speech and my proclamation were not with plausible words of wisdom" (2:4). The foolishness of the cross is preached through "the foolishness of our proclamation" (1:21)! Compared with the kind of speeches the Corinthians desired from their great orators, Christian preaching (as Paul defines it), both in terms of its form and content, is a foolish declaration of God's love for the world in Jesus Christ.

Paul knows the irony of the Corinthians' love for the status associated with eloquent wisdom. Most of them were not born to the upper classes; they were not considered powerful and wise (1:26–31). It is precisely the upside-down nature of God's plan of salvation that allows them to be among the chosen. They have no room to boast in human achievement (1:28–29). Paul's comments raise the issue of class distinctions as they relate to this and other community problems. If "not many" of the Corinthians are from the upper classes, then the implication is that some are. In fact, Gaius, a man baptized by Paul (1:14), is probably a wealthy Roman freedman, the same Gaius Paul describes as being a host for "the whole church" (Romans 16:23). And Crispus, whom Paul also baptized (1:14), is most certainly the synagogue ruler referred to in Acts 18:8. Is it possible that some of the Corinthians' tensions about leadership have their origin in conflict between classes, because members of the higher classes would have the training in and presumably a greater appreciation of rhetoric? Yet in 1:26–31 it is precisely members of the lower classes that Paul chides for their improper pursuit of rhetorical wisdom. Paul gives us no clear answers here, but certainly class diversity is a hallmark of the Corinthian church, and such diversity does play a role in later community issues (see especially 11:17–34). At the very least, Paul's words in 1:26–31 challenge status-quo definitions of class. If the so-called weak and lowly have been chosen by God, then they have a new status, even though the world may not recognize it, and they no longer need to seek the empowerment that comes from their association with rhetorically gifted preachers. Paul is intimating what he will make more obvious later in the letter: that Christian community radically challenges the world's ranking of human beings.

Paul's argument does recognize the Corinthians' desire for wisdom and power: he emphasizes that the cross of Jesus Christ has become their wisdom and power (1:17–18, 24–25; 2:4, 6–16, and so on). This wisdom is rightly defined as the righteousness, sanctification, and redemption that come in Christ (1:30). Paul's words are important because they show that the power and wisdom associated with preaching come through Christ's sacrifice on the cross and through the empowerment of the Spirit (2:4–5) rather than through the persuasive speech of the orator. Ultimately, Paul says, it is God's Spirit who gives understanding (2:10–13); thus, true understanding comes to those who are spiritually mature (2:6). The wise at Corinth must be shocked to realize that Paul considers them, the very ones who so desire wisdom, to be infants (3:1). Wisdom ultimately comes to those who "have the mind of Christ" (2:16).

This discussion of the importance of the Spirit in the hearing process follows logically from what I think is Paul's most problematic statement about preaching in this section. Paul says that when he came to Corinth, he did not come in lofty words or wisdom but "decided to know nothing among you except Jesus Christ, and him crucified" (2:2). Does this mean that when Paul was in their midst his sermons consisted entirely of the barest confession about the death and resurrection of Jesus? And was this an intentional strategy based, as some would have it, on the failure of his more contextual approach in his previous stop, at Athens (Acts 17:16–34)? Paul's intention to know nothing among the Corinthians except Christ crucified could well be seen as an affirmation of sermons whose content is very limited and that lack illustrations, personal testimony, logical development and conclusions, and even interpretation of Scripture! Coming after his many negative statements about human eloquence, Paul's words in 2:2 appear to call for the abolition of sermons as we know them.

Ironically, it is Paul's own rhetorical strategy that helps us respond to these questions. Consistent with the methods of his day, Paul regularly uses hyperbole or overstatement to make his point (see, for instance, his satirical assessment of the Corinthians in 4:8–10 and his earthy comment about his opponents in Galatians 5:12). It makes no sense to assume that when Paul came to Corinth the content of his sermons was limited to a narrow christological focus. As a congregation of new believers, the Corinthians would have needed instruction on an immense variety of topics. And Paul's letters, especially the very passage we are studying, indicate that he had a rhetorical arsenal that would have made his sermons sophisticated. It would be exciting to hear 1:17–2:5 preached. Running throughout is the irony found in the contrast between human wisdom and God's foolishness. Paul uses Scripture (1:19) and questions (1:20) effectively. He appeals to the Corinthians' own existential situation (1:26–31) and reminds his hearers of his experience in their midst (2:1–5). Each paragraph has a cadence that builds to a powerful concluding statement (1:25, 28–29, 2:2). Paul is certainly able and willing to turn a phrase. The critique found in 2 Corinthians 10:10—"His letters are weighty and strong, but his bodily presence is weak"—makes one wonder if people in Corinth criticized Paul's preaching skills primarily because of his delivery or appearance. He admits that he came to the Corinthians in "weakness and in fear and in much trembling,"

(1 Corinthians 2:3) and that he has some physical malady, a "thorn . . . in the flesh" (2 Corinthians 12:7).

Paul did not preach only "Christ and him crucified." In part, he writes as he does to defend his preaching as a legitimate way to proclaim the good news. Hyperbole allows Paul to dramatically distinguish his preaching from that of other, more "acceptable" preachers. But we must continue to remind ourselves that the main reason Paul writes is to instruct his congregation at Corinth and to help its members grow. Paul wants them to become mature hearers of the Word, to move from milk to solid food (3:2). Paul uses hyperbole effectively to teach the Corinthians about their responsibility in hearing the sermon. Paul writes that preaching must be done in a way that emphasizes its most essential purpose, Jesus Christ and his cross. He wants the Corinthians to come to the proclaimed Word aware of the limitations of both the sermon and the preacher and yet confident that the Spirit will work in them to reveal God's power and wisdom. Paul uses hyperbole in a way that both honestly reflects the essential nature of his preaching and startles the people into hearing an important truth.

1 Corinthians 3–4

The concluding chapters in this first unit of thought move the reader back to the comprehensive problem, divisions within the Corinthian church. One's view of preaching inevitably becomes a community issue because it affects how church leaders are perceived. Having defined the function of sermon and preacher, Paul now proceeds to give a definition of Christian leadership. He and Apollos are God's servants, planting and watering, working together in a common task (3:5–9). The work of the servant is not unimportant: it is through servants that the Corinthians came to believe (3:5), and those who are called to be God's servants will receive their reward (3:8, 14) and have strict standards to follow (Paul changes the image to that of *builders* in 3:10–15 and *stewards* in 4:2). But Paul makes it clear that it is "only God who gives the growth" (3:7). This means that the Corinthians' attachment to their leaders is misplaced. They are boasting in human leaders when their boast should be in Christ and the riches of his salvation (3:21–23). Their love of Greco-Roman rhetoric made them seek human wisdom and eloquent heroes, when in reality their leaders are simply fellow servants. Ironically, what they sought in oratory they have already received in Jesus Christ: "For all things are yours" (3:21).

In the process of talking about leaders, Paul introduces several metaphors for Christian community. What does it mean to be God's field (3:5–9), God's building (3:10–15), or God's temple (3:16–17)? The first two images are used primarily as a context for discussing the responsibility of Christian leaders. But the images also invite the hearer to reflect on the unity of the community and the fact that it is an object of God's concern. A field has many plants that, when given the divine growth Paul speaks of, yield a common harvest. The community as building has a common foundation in Jesus Christ; the image implies the interdependence of Christians as they form a solid structure (cf. 14:5, 12, 26). The image of the temple strongly emphasizes God's ownership and protection of the community. The church at Corinth is indwelled by the Holy Spirit and is holy. Paul severely warns those who would tamper with the community God has blessed: "If anyone destroys God's temple, God will destroy that person" (3:17). Together the three metaphors form a powerful affirmation not only of Christian community in general but also of the Corinthian church in particular. Coming as they do after the depiction of the Corinthians as "infants" (3:1), these metaphors are a classic example of Paul's understanding of the paradox of life in the Christian community; because we do not always function as we should, as a community we constantly need to be reminded of what we already are in God's eyes.

Paul concludes this section of 1 Corinthians by satirizing the congregation's pretensions (4:8–13) and by reminding them that they are his children in the gospel (4:14–21). Verses 8–13 are perhaps the sharpest satire found in any of Paul's letters. The Corinthians' assumption that the human wisdom they so prize makes them rich and like kings (4:8) is a reflection of philosophical thought of that day on the value of wisdom. Paul is also making a comment about their spiritual pretentiousness, especially their assumption that they have been richly empowered by the Holy Spirit, an issue that will surface several times in this letter (see 12:21–25). Paul's contrast between their attitude and his own life of suffering and service shows again how poorly they understand the Christian life. The apostle drives his point home by illustrating what the foolishness of the cross has meant in his own life (4:11–13), engaging in a kind of "boasting" that he will use again in 2 Corinthians 10–13. Finally, Paul threatens disciplinary action if the Corinthians do not come to their senses (4:21: "Am I to come to you with a stick?"). Reestablishing his authority is important if this letter is to have any impact at all. It is obvious that Paul sees no tension between what he has just said about the danger of idolizing leaders and the kind of authority he can claim for himself as the founding father of this congregation. A flawed understanding of preachers and leaders can destroy community, but Paul never concludes that leadership is unnecessary.

Paul's description of himself as father and the Corinthians as beloved children (4:14–15) points to another important image of community, this one never explicitly stated—that of the church as "family." Here, because of Paul's need to defend his authority, we see an unusual application of the term *father*. Paul is the Corinthians' "father through the gospel"; that is, he is the one who led them to the Christian faith. His love for them is like a father's: he hopes to admonish, not shame them (4:14), and he offers himself as an example (4:16). Typically Paul speaks instead of God as Father and Christians as joint heirs of Christ and children of God (see Galatians 3:29–4:7 and Romans 8:14–17, and notice the typical "God our Father" in the salutation, 1 Corinthians 1:3). Consequently, Paul addresses his fellow Christians as brothers and sisters and fellow children. We are siblings in God's family, and as members of a common family we are expected to love one another (chapter 13) and be responsible for one another in the faith (see 8:7–13). The concept of family is always close to the surface in Paul's writings and is one of the key images of community found in his letters.

As we have seen, Paul's message in 1 Corinthians 1–4 is a strong reaction to a dangerous situation; the Christian community at Corinth is being split into factions that are based on improper attachments to certain leaders. Their attitude has arisen primarily out of a faulty understanding of preaching. The Corinthians want their preachers to be like their beloved orators, displaying human wisdom through the logic, persuasion, and beauty of fine rhetoric. Paul's response, an impassioned statement about the implications of the cross of Jesus Christ and the function of leaders as servants, is remarkably relevant for us as we struggle with community problems in the modern church.

Paul's Words for the Contemporary Community

Seeking Servant Leaders

After I make a few initial comments about this passage in a Sunday morning Bible study class, it is not unusual for my adult students to lapse into silence, numbed by the painful relevance of it all. When they recover, almost everyone has a story to tell about leadership problems and how their community was strained or even split because of them. Certain dilemmas are all too typical. Part of a congregation feels that its associate pastor is a more capable and energetic leader than its aging senior pastor. They build up their chosen minister and create resentment in the community until a crisis is reached and the whole group leaves to start its own church. Or the current pastor is evaluated in light of the abilities of a capable former pastor who sometimes served many years previously, and those who find the new pastor lacking feel resentment toward those who affirm his ministry. Often tensions occur in a community when people line up behind strong lay leaders, elders, or board members who are articulate visionaries or who have the backing of a powerful family in the church. It is not uncommon for people to talk about being mesmerized by a talented pastor and how this adoration led to an unhealthy emphasis on the minister's gifts rather than on the gifts present in the larger congregation. The examples go on and on. We have no problem relating to the passion Paul expresses on this issue!

How do the apostle's words in chapters 1–4 help us understand Christian leadership, especially as it stands in relationship to Christian community? Obviously we need to affirm the ministry of our leaders, just as Paul expects the Corinthians to affirm his groundbreaking work among them. What then constitutes an improper attitude toward our leaders? Paul's criticism of the Corinthians for their boasting is an important clue (see 1:28–31; 3:21; 4:7). The term *boast* (*kauchaomai*) is theologically significant for Paul, because what people boast about offers important insight into their relationship with God. There is a legitimate kind of boasting for Christians—boasting in God (1:31; Romans 5:11), in the cross (Galatians 6:14), in our hope (Romans 5:2), even in our sufferings (2 Corinthians 11:16–33; Romans 5:3). But there is another kind of boasting that Paul is very wary of: boasting in the human enterprise in a way that denies the grace of God. In Romans 3:27 Paul says that boasting is excluded because we are justified by faith, not by works. Boasting indicates an attitude toward God that is prideful about human achievement and fails to see that salvation is entirely a gift from God (Romans 4:2). In 1 Corinthians 1–4 Paul says that the people are boasting in their leaders, but that this boasting reflects the same kind of misunderstanding about who saves whom. In 3:21–23 the various groups are told not to boast in human leaders because "all things are yours." These leaders are not the source of their salvation and can add nothing to its glory. The same theme is echoed in 4:7. Speaking of their salvation, Paul asks, "Why do you boast as if it were not a gift?" And in 1:26–29 Paul shows how God's upside-down standards, even the very choice of these lowly Corinthians, make any boast on their part ridiculous.

We improperly value our leaders when we boast in them, when we confuse what they offer with what can be received only through God. To boast in a Christian leader is to emphasize to the extreme a church's dependence on the wisdom, vision, charisma, and instruction of an individual pastor or lay leader. Our attitude toward leadership is a problem when in the pastoral selection process, we believe that if we can just call the right person, everything in our church will be turned around. It is a problem if church members feel there is no reason to attend worship when the pastor is on vacation or if it is assumed that the pastor must be present for any committee meeting to be legitimate. There is a problem with our attitude toward leadership if church members are so enamored of the gifts of their leader that they forget their own, or if this infatuation with one leader causes them to reject all others. A boasting attitude relative to our leaders is a threat to Christian community because it produces amnesia about God as our common source of empowerment and leads to conflict as we struggle to find a perfect human replacement.

What attracts people to their Christian leaders? In the church at Corinth the attraction is human wisdom, especially the kind of wisdom that manifests itself in fine rhetoric. The people seek leaders whose eloquence and all that it involves brings status to the group with which they are associated. Of course this is the world's definition, and that is why Paul rejects it. Paul shows how the cross of Jesus Christ turns the world's standards upside down. The foolishness of the gospel means that we seek leaders who are defined not by their human wisdom, but by their service to God. Christian leaders are servants.

The community conflict I so frequently hear spoken of has its origin in people's desire for an illegitimate kind of leadership more than anything else. Our problem is exactly like that of the Corinthians: we seek leaders on the basis of society's definition of excellence and use them to empower and protect the interests of our group. So we are attracted to authoritative personalities and self-assured, articulate, intelligent, even beautiful leaders not primarily because we think those characteristics will make them effective servants, but because we hope some of these leaders' status and power will rub off on us. It is not uncommon for Christians to be attracted to their church leaders in almost the same way they are attracted to political celebrities or movie stars. The church too often becomes a cult of personality. Paul's words and actions indicate that a Christian leader does have authority, but the genuine authority of the servant is often less appealing than other, more glamorous kinds of power.

I have been speaking about leadership as a congregational responsibility because that is Paul's point of view in chapters 1–4. He never blames the personalities listed in 1:12 for the divisions that have occurred, although what he says is an implicit warning for leaders. We all know of instances in which congregations became groupies because their pastors tried to be gurus. What is amazing is that Paul does not even try to claim his own group. He de-emphasizes any link he might have with them on the basis of baptism (1:13–16), and his warning about seeking wise leaders applies to his followers as well. Paul knows that their loyalty toward him is illegitimate because it produces jealousy and quarreling in the church (3:3–4).

Paul's approach here provides an important model for today's Christian leaders. We who are leaders must refuse to cultivate a following that has its impulse in the desire for wisdom rather than servanthood.

This first section of 1 Corinthians gives a radical definition of leadership that shapes our understanding of Christian community in a significant way. In the cross of Jesus Christ the world's standards have been turned upside down. Instead of so-called "wise" leaders, we are told to seek leaders who are servants of God (3:5–9; 4:1). Above all, Christian leaders owe their allegiance to the One who has called them to service. In Jesus Christ they have been given an assigned task (3:5) and have become "stewards of God's mysteries" (4:1); in him their work will be judged (4:2–5). One of the gravest threats to Christian community occurs when people believe their leader is theirs to manipulate, whether through adulation or criticism or, too often, the paycheck. It has become so easy in the modern church to forget the high calling of our pastors and simply treat them as employees. Both Paul's words and actions tell us that our leaders must have a clear sense of their calling as servants of God: they must have an authority in Christ that makes them independent of the various whims of their congregations.

Paul also uses the servant image to relativize the importance of leaders in comparison to the larger community. If we think of servant leaders in relationship to the images of the church Paul employs in this section, their humble status becomes obvious. Servants who labor in the community as a *field* know that they are less important than the common harvest and certainly less important than God who gives the growth (3:5–9). Servants who construct the community as a *building* humbly recognize the common foundation we share in Jesus Christ and their responsibility to build upon it and no other (3:10–15). Those who serve in the community as a *temple* realize that it is holy and blessed and that their service must uphold the sanctity of the church, not divide or destroy it (3:16–17). Finally, servants who nurture the community as a *family* prize the love that binds them together with other family members, recognizing that their task is only one of many that holds the family network together. Each of these illustrations makes clear that following a Christian leader who is a servant means leaving behind a divisive reliance on the human enterprise and humbly pursuing that which nourishes and builds up the larger group.

Responsible Hearers

More than anything else, the specific task that defines excellence in leadership for the Corinthians is preaching. They reflect the typical Greco-Roman view about the speaker and the speaker's responsibility.

It is the orator's task to persuade and entertain the audience, and, if this is done well, it is the orator who receives the adulation. The audience responds to the speaker's strategy and ultimately sits in judgment of the speaker's words, but how the speech is heard and interpreted is the responsibility of the speaker. Paul's message for the Christian audience as it hears God's Word preached is radical in its context because it gives the hearers an important responsibility: to listen in a way that is sympathetic with and seeks out the message being proclaimed. The Corinthians are not just passive hearers, waiting to be convinced by the most able speaker. They are Christians who know what the essential message is and who, in their desire to hear this message, can relativize society's definitions of excellent speech. Paul assumes that the Corinthians are able to recognize the Word of God when they hear it. They are able to distinguish it from what is merely the speaker's art.

The parallel between the Corinthians' situation and ours is amazing. Preaching is almost always mentioned when conflict around pastoral leadership is mentioned. In fact, when I lead discussions about leadership and community, many people assume that preaching is the only issue involved! Churches both select pastors and choose to like or dislike them primarily on the basis of their ability to preach. Paul's words about preaching are important for us because they relativize the task and person of the preacher. Not everything depends on the one standing in the pulpit. The congregation has the responsibility to discern the Word rather than seek the eloquent wisdom of the speaker. Those who do discern the Word are the "mature" hearers Paul discusses in 2:6–16. The wisdom they receive is a gift of the Spirit (2:10–13). The purpose of the sermon is not fulfilled in the preaching, but in the proclamation that is heard and lived.

The problem Paul must confront in Corinth illustrates something that is invariably true: society dictates how we define excellence in communication. In the world of the Corinthians, Greco-Roman rhetoric sets the standards, and it is on these standards that the Corinthians are tempted to evaluate their preachers. What are the standards for communication excellence in our world? My guess is that a typical American understanding of the ideal in communication is based especially on what we see in our movie and TV stars, news commentators, and comedians. A good speaker is easy to look at, has an authoritative yet caring voice, and speaks succinctly, factually, entertainingly, and with a good supply of humor. The point Paul is making in 1 Corinthians 1–4, however, is that when Christians listen to sermons they should not simply borrow the world's standards of evaluation. Paul makes it clear that everything about the sermon, both in its content and its form, is opposite of the world's definition of wisdom. Preaching the gospel is foolishness; it is a countercultural activity. Is listening to sermons not then also foolishness, a radical, world-denying act? Listening for God's Word, as Paul defines it, calls into question status-quo expectations of an audience. If the Corinthians are asked to question the value of eloquent wisdom, what are we being asked to question? In what ways has society fooled us about the nature of the sermon?

For me, the most helpful thing Paul says on this issue is his clear statement that Christian hearers must avoid an attitude toward proclamation that allows us to see preachers as either heroes or misfits. In light of God's radical act in Jesus Christ and the ongoing work of the Spirit, we must not "claim" or boast in a certain preacher as if she or he were the focus of the proclamation. Christians are not the preacher's groupies. We do not go to the sermon as if to a performance, that we might revel in the speaker's charm and beauty and collect a few more memorable phrases.

All of us know of instances in which a church's failure to grasp the proper relationship between sermon and preacher resulted in broken community. Are there other ways in which how we listen to sermons stresses or divides Christian community? Some people, for instance, always approach the sermon with a personal or interpretive agenda. Their pet issue becomes the hermeneutical key to every word that issues from the pastor's mouth, and the resulting slant on what is said leads to conflict. Others assume they have a special gift for applying sermons in the life of the church, a gift that they feel empowers them and sets them apart. They are like the Christians Paul addresses in 1 Corinthians 12–14. Certainly the link between hearing the Word and forming community deserves more attention than it has been given. Perhaps more community-splitting issues have their origin in the congregation's attitude toward sermon and preacher than we think.

Defined by the Cross

The Corinthians are probably not preaching a heretical Christology, but their attachment to the eloquent wisdom of their preachers indicates a serious christological problem. Their actions are not without theological impact. Paul's strong christological response (1:17–31) to what might appear to be a simple misunderstanding about preaching shows how seriously the apostle is treating this issue. Paul's statements about the foolishness of the cross and how God turns the world's standards upside down are meant to define the agenda for the entire letter. Paul's Christology of reversal will impact each of the community barriers he addresses.

That Paul wants to link the message of the cross directly with a proper understanding of Christian community is clearly shown in 1:26–31. After discussing the relationship between the cross and the proclamation in 1:17–25, Paul continues his argument in verses 26–31 by reminding the Corinthians who they are as the people of God. Two things are especially important. First of all, Paul affirms that the Corinthians have been called or chosen by God (1:26–28). Community has its origin in an act of God, who seeks us and chooses us. This is the most essential thing that we as Christians share. And second, the God who chooses us is defined most fully by the work of Christ on the cross, an act the world did not anticipate and that the world considers foolish. This God is consistently foolish, because the people he chooses are the weak, the lowly, and the despised (1:27–28). Paul employs this selection of the weak as a deliberate way of challenging the world's powerful: God chose his people "to shame the wise," (v. 27); "to shame the strong," (v. 27); and "to reduce to nothing things that are" (v. 28). Christian community, Paul is telling us, will be different. Both its inception and its understanding of who belongs are unlike anything found in the world.

Paul's message and his poetic energy in 1:26–31 remind me of Old Testament passages, some of them used in the New Testament, that speak of God's calling and protection of Israel. Hannah's song (1 Samuel 2:1–10), loosely quoted in the Magnificat (Luke 1:46–55), tells how God reverses the status of the lowly and makes them "sit with princes and inherit a seat of honor" (1 Samuel 2:8). The author of 1 Peter uses Hosea 2:23 and Exodus 19:5–6 to explain to his gentile audience how God has selected them in an unexpected way:

> But you are a chosen race, a royal priesthood, a holy nation, God's own people, in order that you may proclaim the mighty acts of him who called you out of darkness into his marvelous light.
>
> Once you were not a people,
>   but now you are God's people;
> once you had not received mercy,
>   but now you have received mercy (1 Peter 2:9–10).

God's surprising call of enslaved and lowly Israel is parallel to what is now happening to Christians on the basis of the cross.

What does the message of the cross mean for community in the modern church? It defines us in every way, and we will be pursuing nuances of this question in the chapters that follow. Perhaps we could begin here simply by reminding ourselves what it means to feel the tension between this understanding of community and the kind the world is constantly trying to force upon us. The author of 1 Peter understands the tension with the world implicit in his description of the Christian community; in the very next line he calls Christians "aliens" and "exiles" (1 Peter 2:11). First Corinthians 1–4 affirms that those who accept this radical definition of community will not be considered wise by the world's standards. Even worse, this tension may enter the life of the church. Do we really dare to lift up the lowly in our churches and declare that old, worldly ways of assessing the value of people are being set aside? Are we able to acknowledge that the unpredictable God of the cross is the author of our community? How will we deal with the tension between what we know we should be as a community and what our actions indicate about us?

In *An American Childhood*, Annie Dillard describes her youth in the Shadyside Presbyterian Church of Pittsburgh. Her story rings true to those who have felt similar conflict. As a teenager she saw her church as a place filled with pretense, pious self-interest, and meaningless tradition.

> Nothing so inevitably blackened my heart as an obligatory Sunday at Shadyside Presbyterian Church: the sight of orphan-girl Liz's "Jesus" tricked out in guilt; the minister's Britishy accent; the putative hypocrisy of my parents, who forced me to go, though they did not; the putative hypocrisy of the expensive men and women who did go. I knew enough of the Bible to damn these people to hell, citing chapter and verse.[5]

It was a church where long-time members grew "not close, but respectful," their primary purpose in being at church to "accumulate dignity." The pastor's radio ministry was apparently directed toward working-class people, "Alaskan lumberjacks and fisherman," as she recalls, but she doubts that anyone who showed up wearing a lumberjack shirt would have been allowed to enter the church. She remembers thinking that "maybe the ushers were really bouncers."[6]

There is a terrible irony in that the very body that proclaims a countercultural message about community appears least able to live it. But there is a second irony as well. Even as a teenager Dillard was able to discern that God was working in the midst of this stuffy, exclusive congregation. Several pages later Dillard writes of the amazement she felt when she sensed God's special presence among this group of hypocrites during the Lord's Supper:

> The ushers and their trays had vanished. The people had taken Communion. No one moved. The organist hushed. All the men's heads were bent— black, white, red, yellow, and brown. The men sat absolutely still. Almost

all the women's heads were bent down, too, and some few tilted back. Some hats wagged faintly from side to side. All the people seemed scarcely to breathe.

I was alert enough now to feel, despite myself, some faint, thin stream of spirit braiding forward from the pews. Its flawed and fragile rivulets pooled far beyond me at the altar. I felt, or saw, its frail strands rise to the wide tower ceiling, and mass in the gold mosaic's dome.

The gold tesserae scattered some spirit like light back over the cavernous room, and held some of it, like light, in its deep curve. Christ drifted among the floating sandstone ledges and deep, absorbent skies.[7]

This is the same tension Paul expresses as he reminds the Corinthians what it means to be a Christian community. Because they reflect the world, they are infants, fleshy, a quarreling and divided church. But because the God of the cross is working among them, they are God's chosen, God's temple, and God's family. To be a community of the cross means that we are set apart by God, who has radical plans for us. These plans will challenge society's status quo and may well bring conflict. Community formation, at least as Paul imagines it, is not the pleasant activity many think it will be. And yet Paul's words are amazingly hopeful in their clear affirmation of what the church already is, in spite of its problems. In a real sense the entire letter of 1 Corinthians is an exhortation to be communally what we already are in Jesus Christ.

Community
and Ethical Boundaries

1 Corinthians 5–6

Hearing the opening chapters of Paul's letter must have been an unpleasant experience for the church at Corinth. The Corinthians probably expected Paul's words to be a simple response to their most recent letter to him, but he delays giving a direct response until chapter 7. Instead they discover that Paul has heard a great deal about their current situation (things they had intentionally left out of their correspondence?) and that he considers these developments to be a threat not only to his authority, but more importantly to their integrity as a Christian community. Imagine the squirming and even the anger generated as the Corinthians realize that this letter will be much more than pious small talk.

We in the modern church squirm as well, especially when we are confronted with the next two chapters in Paul's letter. The apostle makes it very clear that immorality and a failure to distinguish between the church and the world form a significant barrier to community. Because many of us in mainline denominations have never seen our churches discipline members or prescribe ethical boundaries, we are torn between the extremes of rejecting Paul's words as antiquated on the one hand and thinking that the modern church has failed to hear a clear biblical teaching on the other. We become uncomfortable when someone calls into question our easy alliance with American culture. Even a superficial reading of 1 Corinthians 5–6 warns us that the boundaries we have erected between church and world, if they exist at all, may have to be redefined. These chapters bother us, perhaps most of all because they challenge our common assumption that the ethical life of individual believers has nothing to do with Christian community.

1 Corinthians 5

Paul is astounded that a member of the Corinthian church is living with his stepmother in an incestuous relationship considered taboo even in the often amoral Greco-Roman world (5:1). Yet it quickly becomes obvious that Paul's primary concern is not this audacious sin but the church's callous attitude toward it and the resulting danger to the community. Instead of mourning over this corruption in their midst, the church is arrogant (5:2) and boastful (5:6); Paul employs the same words he uses in chapters 1–4 to describe their attitude. What accounts for this arrogance? It could be that they are overly confident that this sin will not affect them as individuals and as a community. As wise, gifted, and empowered Christians, surely they can live godly lives in spite of the presence of this unrepentant sinner! It is even possible that the church is boasting *because of* its acceptance of this man. We know that Paul's message emphasizes freedom from the law and that the Corinthians knew how to push that freedom to its extreme. Paul quotes them as saying, "All things are lawful for me," a stance he immediately challenges: "but not all things are beneficial" (6:12; cf. 10:23). Perhaps this is a church that has not simply failed to exercise discipline, but that considers freedom and the absence of discipline to be part of its theological stance. Perhaps they are proud of their radical freedom, proud of being the "liberal church" that accepts everyone, including those who sin in ways that even society would condemn.[1]

Whether the Corinthians are boasting in spite of or because of the presence of this man and his sin, Paul rejects their stance because it fails to exhibit understanding of how one person's immorality can affect the entire community. In what must be a real test of his authority, Paul tells the church at Corinth to excommunicate the man (5:3–5). When they have assembled together, guided by Paul's spirit and empowered by Jesus Christ, the church is to "hand this man over to Satan for the destruction of the flesh, so that his spirit may be saved in the day of the Lord" (vv. 4–5). It is unfortunate that Paul uses such ambiguous language here. A common interpretation, that Paul assumes that physical death will result from excommunication, has only served to make people more wary of church discipline. Actually, insight into how Paul is using the words *Satan*, *flesh*, and *spirit* reveals that the pronouncement is significantly less harsh. In the dualistic cosmology of Paul, to be dismissed from the church is to be delivered into the realm of Satan. And if *flesh* and *spirit* form a contrasting word pair as they typically do in Paul's writings, *flesh* refers to the man's sinful nature and not his physical body. The desired result of the man's exclusion from the church is that his sinful nature or "old self" might be destroyed (cf. Romans 6:5–11) so that he might be saved in the end, "in the day of the Lord." Still we wish that Paul would tell us more about church discipline in addition to explaining that it might ultimately be remedial. Exactly what process should be used by the church to determine the person's guilt? Paul is hurrying to get to his real concern, the way the community is affected by this illicit relationship (5:6–8), and he is spare in his practical advice about discipline in the church.

Paul illustrates the threat the undisciplined member poses to the community by using what is probably a common proverb: "Do you not know that a little leaven leavens the whole lump"(5:6)? Like Jesus' parables, Paul's saying lends itself to a variety of interpretations. Part of the ambiguity of the proverb lies in the term *leaven*. In its nonreligious usage, *leaven* can symbolize either impurity (the small piece of dough kept to leaven the next batch of bread can spoil) or the infectious process (cf. Matthew 13:33; Mark 8:15; see also Paul's use of the proverb in Galatians 5:9). The mention of leaven reminds Paul of its religious significance for the Jewish people, and verses 7 and 8 are an amplification of the proverb based upon the rituals of Passover. Paul alludes to both the Feast of Unleavened Bread and the Paschal Lamb and in the process refocuses the proverb in terms of the contrast between old and new. While it is clear that the proverb and Paul's discussion of it point to a relationship between the one and the many, it is not obvious exactly what Paul is intending to say about how the undisciplined member affects the community.

The primary message of this section of the letter is that the church must be distinct from the world, both in terms of its morality (chapter 5; 6:9–20) and in the way it handles internal disputes (6:1–8). Paul's allusion to Passover and to Christ as our Paschal Lamb emphasizes this separateness. Like Israel as it was about to flee Egypt, the church has been marked by the blood of the Lamb, and it too stands as God's chosen and under his protection.[2] It is hard not to understand Paul's words about the holiness of the church in 3:16–17 as an anticipation of the discussion in these chapters, especially because the apostle now addresses how immorality pollutes not only one's body as the temple of the Holy Spirit (6:18–20) but also one's relationship with Christ (6:15). It has been suggested that 1 Corinthians 5 is a midrash (interpretation) based on Deuteronomy 23:1–8.[3] The passage in Deuteronomy lists those who may not enter the holy temple because of their sin or uncleanness. Interestingly, the passage in Deuteronomy also appears following a prohibition about a man having sexual relations with his stepmother (22:30). If the Christian community is holy, as Paul asserts that it is, then lack of discipline affects that holiness. The community is leavened in the sense that both its distinctiveness and its ability to represent God in the world are compromised. The latter is very important to Paul, who defines the church in terms of involvement beyond its own community (5:9–13).

An interesting and related interpretation sees the community affected corporately by the acts of the sinning member. Several Old Testament stories show how the sins of individuals or small groups are held against the entire community (Exodus 16:22–28; Deuteronomy 29:19–25; Joshua 22:11–18). Moreover, the word Paul uses for "mourn" in verse 2 (*pentheō*) functions elsewhere in his letters (2 Corinthians 12:21) and in the Septuagint to refer to mourning on the basis of one's conviction of sin.[4] Perhaps Paul is enjoining the Corinthian community to mourn not because they have been shamed or because they will lose a brother, but because God holds the whole batch of dough responsible for the sin of the unleavened member, in which case they all need to repent.

The most obvious interpretation of the proverb in 5:6 is that the sin of one infects others; contamination occurs in the sense that others will be encouraged to sin because of the presence and example of the undisciplined member. As we will see in chapters 8–10, Paul is acutely aware of how people may be caused to stumble because of the actions of others. If Paul is concerned about modeling in the so-called gray areas of the ethical life—the issue of eating meat offered to idols, for example— how much more will he be concerned about the impact a clear violation of Christian morality will have upon the entire community. Leaven is a symbol for how a small thing can quickly and thoroughly contaminate the whole. In this case church discipline is related to community in that it functions to safeguard the moral integrity of the group.

First Corinthians 5:7 is a classic example of what scholars sometimes call the Pauline "indicative/imperative." The concepts of the indicative and the imperative, two grammatical moods, are helpful in describing Paul's understanding of the relationship between, on the one hand, what we already are as saved people and, on the other hand, how we need to be motivated to live in a way that is consistent with this saved status. A sentence in the indicative mood makes a statement of fact. The Pauline indicative is a clear declaration of what Christ has done for us and that we are already God's people. A sentence in the imperative mood issues a command. The Pauline imperative is an exhortation for believers to live the Christian life. This command and the motivation to follow it always have their origin in the indicative; they flow out of the free gift of salvation that is already ours in Christ. The need for the command reflects the paradox of the Christian life, the tension between our new life in Christ and the reality of our fallenness.

In 5:7 Paul exhorts the Corinthians to be a new, pure batch of dough, a community that is willing to discipline itself and take seriously its moral standards. But immediately following this imperative Paul reminds the Corinthians: "you really are unleavened." As if this clear indicative were not enough, he reminds them that the blood of Christ, their Paschal Lamb, has marked them as a distinct and holy community. It is very important for Paul that he clarify the motivation for the kind of ethical uniqueness he is advocating. With this foundation, the imperative is not a burden, but a call to delight in the community's celebration of the new life: "Therefore, let us celebrate the festival, not with the old yeast . . . but with the unleavened bread of sincerity and truth" (v. 8).

The next paragraph (5:9–13) reflects Paul's anticipation that the Corinthians will misinterpret what he has said about the moral separateness of the church. Both here and in a previous letter (see v. 9), Paul has stated that the Corinthians are not to associate with those who continue to live in immorality. Perhaps that means they should form a sect and isolate themselves from the world as much as possible! But Paul makes it clear that he is not telling them to dissociate themselves from the immoral in the world (v. 10). Although here the only reason he gives them for maintaining their presence in the world is that it would be impossible to avoid such contact ("since you would then need to go out of the world"), surely the apostle also has in mind the church's missionary activity. In chapter 9, for instance, Paul uses himself as an example of one who daringly "became all things to all people," a kind of incarnation in the world for the sake of the gospel (9:22). The danger Paul is warning against is not that of the Christian community entering the world, but that of the world entering the Christian community. The Corinthians are to shun members of the Christian family if they continue to live in a way that reflects the world (5:11). Sometimes exclusion of an unrepentant member is necessary if the purity and distinctiveness of the community is to be preserved.

1 Corinthians 6

The boundaries that separate the community from the world indicate that Christians should not concern themselves with judging those on the "outside" (5:12). Maintaining a morally distinct community is certainly enough of a task. Paul's reference to judging must have reminded him of a practice among the Corinthians that was equally repulsive: allowing non-Christians to judge lawsuits between those inside the community (6:1–8). Christians clearly have the authority to handle such disputes. The best evidence of this for Paul is that the saints will take part in the final judgment, even judging the angels (6:2–3; cf.

Matthew 19:28). Surely the Corinthians are wise enough for this task, Paul explains, in a not-so-subtle stab at those who champion human wisdom (v. 5). But Paul's most important reason for rejecting non-Christian mediation is simply that the Christian community has standards that are incompatible with those of the world. Even the practice of bringing lawsuits is to be challenged. It represents an attitude of self-preservation that is not consistent with the message of the cross. The world would never understand the kind of sacrifice for the benefit of the community that frees Christians to be voluntarily wronged or defrauded (v. 7). Having non-Christians judge lawsuits between Christians allows the world's standards to invade and pollute the church in a way that is very similar to the impact of the immoral person described in chapter 5.

Recently scholars have speculated that there may be an additional reason for Paul's wariness of the Roman courts. We know that the court system was biased in favor of upper-class citizens, those who could afford legal representation. Judges and juries were drawn from the elite and were naturally more sympathetic to those of their own class. Bribery was not uncommon. Studies have shown that people from the upper classes were far more apt to bring litigation against those of the lower classes than vice versa.[5] The inability to achieve equal justice under the law may be reflected in verse 8, where Paul says that the Corinthians use lawsuits to "wrong and defraud" fellow Christians. Certainly Paul is aware of class differences (1:26–31) and even class tensions (see especially 11:17–22) among the Christians at Corinth. If the abuse of the poor and powerless at the hands of the legal system lies behind Paul's argument in 6:1–8, then we have a concrete reason why allowing the world's standards to enter the church is so unacceptable in this case. In Christian community, members of the lower classes also have been called and empowered (1:26–31), and as we shall see, they too have rights (chapters 8–10) and important gifts (chapter 12). As Paul intimates in 6:6–8, the community is a family in which it is unfitting for siblings to treat each other in such a degrading way (the *brother* in the Greek is translated "believer" in the NRSV, disguising the family language Paul uses here). The kind of arbitration Paul envisions taking place in the church would certainly give lower-class Christians a voice they did not have in the Roman courts. Paul's rejection of the pagan legal system was probably understood by the Corinthians to be a declaration of equality that challenged the standards of their world.

In the final two paragraphs in this section (6:9–11 and 6:12–20) Paul continues to discuss the boundaries that distinguish the ethical lives of Christians from those of non-Christians. Expanding on what he has just said about the specific sins of sexual immorality (5:1–13) and wronging fellow Christians in lawsuits (6:1–8), he gives the Corinthians a list of activities that Christians should recognize as sinful (6:9; cf. 5:11). Once again we have a clear example of Paul's use of the indicative/imperative. The sins mentioned in verse 9 are not simply illustrative of the behavior of those who will not inherit the kingdom of God, but they are also things that Christians are commanded to avoid. "Do not be deceived" (v. 9), Paul says, warning those who might be tempted to live as they once did. This command to live lives that are unstained by the world's standards has its motivation in the cleansing that has already occurred in Jesus Christ. The Corinthians have been washed; that is, they have been sanctified and justified (v. 11). To experience salvation through the foolishness of the cross (1:18–31) means that Christians are expected to have ethical lives that are foolish as well, in the sense that they are so unlike what is typically seen in the world. Paul's use of this list of prohibited activities and his exhortations based upon it are his way of defining Christian community ethically, both in terms of how it is different from the world and especially in terms of normative values that bind one Christian to another. Paul assumes that there should be consensus about what it means to live out one's salvation and that this ethical consensus becomes part of the glue that holds Christian community together.

Paul's words in 6:12–20 graphically illustrate how poorly some in the Corinthian church understand the ethical uniqueness of the Christian life. Once again a particular issue is the focus, this time the use of prostitutes (vv. 15–16). That Christians would practice and defend such immorality seems incredible to us in the modern church until we realize that their behavior would not have been considered unusual in the Hellenistic world. Prostitution was legal, and satisfying one's sexual desires with a prostitute was socially acceptable. This openness to sexual immorality was based, at least in part, on a commonly held view that the physical body was relatively unimportant. Greek religions and philosophies spoke of the immortality of the soul or spirit, but not the resurrection of the body (see Paul's argument in chapter 15), and it was often affirmed that what a person did with her or his body was of no religious consequence.

Paul begins his argument by quoting and then refuting slogans the Corinthians may have been using to justify their behavior (vv. 12–13), slogans that reflect both this typical Hellenistic attitude toward immorality and, interestingly, their distortion of what Paul has said about Christian freedom. Some defend their actions by saying, "All things are lawful for me" (v. 12). These confident Corinthians cannot imagine that their lofty spiritual lives can be affected by something so mundane as the physical body. And had not Paul said that they were free from the law? But Paul's response shows how far afield these Corinthians have gone. Coming as it does after Paul's list of prohibitions in verse 9, the slogan shows how little the Corinthians understand about the ethical absolutes in the Christian life. A Christian community is not a group of individuals doing whatever they please, but people bound together by normative values that grow out of their relationship to Christ. Paul makes it clear that the kind of freedom the Corinthians are practicing is illegitimate because it fails to consider either its impact upon community ("but not all things are beneficial" [v. 12; 10:23]) or the risk of enslavement to certain practices ("but I will not be dominated by anything" [v. 12]).

The next slogan probably extends farther than most English translations indicate. It includes not only the saying that "food is meant for the stomach and the stomach for food" but also the statement that "and God will destroy both one and the other" (v. 13). It is difficult to determine beginnings and endings of quotations when translating from the ancient Greek language, because the Greek has no quotation marks. The latter phrase is probably used by the Corinthians rather than Paul, in light of the negative way it portrays the physical body. The Corinthians are saying, in effect, that the body has natural appetites that might as well be satisfied, because in the end the body will cease to exist anyway. Paul rejects this rationale for participating in sexual immorality by affirming in various ways that God highly values the physical bodies of believers. God raised Jesus Christ from the dead and will raise the bodies of Christians as well (v. 14; cf. chapter 15). Even more, especially in terms of what it means for community, Paul says that our bodies are united with Christ in a way that is akin to the union that occurs in marriage (v. 16b). Our bodies are members of Christ (v. 15); we have become one spirit with him (v. 17). Like the church (3:16), an individual believer's body is a temple of the Holy Spirit (v. 19). This means that those who have sexual relations with prostitutes are joining what is worldly and unholy to Christ himself (v. 15). They are, if one pushes the analogy a bit farther, committing adultery against Christ, the One with whom they have a legitimate union.

Paul's discussion of *body* here is quite different from his well-known use of the term in 12:12–26. Here he is concerned with the sanctity of the individual Christian's physical body; there he uses the body and its many parts as an illustration of the unity and especially diversity of the Christian community. Yet even the present passage, 6:12–20, has important implications for community. If our bodies are united with Christ in a holy union, then by extension we are also united with other Christians who have this relationship with Christ. We share in the body of Christ with other believers. And if immorality affects Christ's body, it must also affect others who are bound to his body, as

Paul clearly states when he writes of leaven and dough in chapter 5. From this linking of individual bodies to Christ it is really only a small step to using the concept of the body of Christ to describe the oneness of all Christians. As Paul says in 12:27, "Now you are the body of Christ and individually members of it" (cf. 10:17: "We who are many are one body"). At the very least Paul is telling the Corinthians that their sins against the physical body are not, as they thought, private or inconsequential. Their actions affect their union with the one who called them into community (1:26–31) and who is the common source of their empowerment.

Paul concludes this section with another indicative/imperative: "For you were bought with a price; therefore glorify God in your body" (v. 20). In the indicative statement Paul invokes the image of a master paying the price to purchase a slave (cf. 7:22–23). In the cross of Jesus Christ the Corinthians have been freed from their slavery to sin and are now servants of their new master (cf. Romans 6:15–22). The imperative statement follows naturally: the Corinthians must glorify God in their bodies. What a difference there is between this command and the Corinthian slogan quoted by Paul in verse 12! The Christian life, especially as it is lived out in community, is not a pursuit of individual freedom. Rather, it is a way of living that recognizes how a person's moral life affects one's relationship both with God and with fellow Christians. Christians glorify God in their bodies when they acknowledge who their new master is and thus live lives that are holy and distinct as people who are intimately involved in community.

Paul's Words for the Contemporary Community

The Disciplining Community

The movie *The Age of Innocence*, based on the Edith Wharton novel of the same name,[6] provides an interesting "secular" parallel to modern Christians' typical reaction to 1 Corinthians 5. The movie is set in the tightly regulated upper-class community of New York City during the 1870s and gives fascinating glimpses at the social life and hierarchy of a bygone era. The story centers on two members of this community, a betrothed and later married man, and a woman separated from her husband and seeking divorce. These two are attracted to each other and try to have an adulterous relationship, but the community makes their affair impossible. Using various means of influence, ranging from guilt to financial pressure to the seating order at their lavish parties, the community enforces its standards.

Movie critics rightly praised the production for its authentic costuming, its grasp of Victorian social life, and its acting. But when they evaluated the theme of the movie, they invariably saw the would-be lovers as victims of a manipulative social structure. They were interpreting the intention of the movie correctly and in a way that was consistent with the modern American valuation of individual freedom. Yet from another point of view, indeed from the point of view of the era in which the movie is set, the community and its disciplining guidance would be understood quite differently. It is entirely possible to see the social pressure put upon the man and the woman as a good thing, both for them and for the community. The lovers are prevented from destroying their lives. The community is able to affirm its standards as a bond that joins its members together.

Like those movie critics, we modern Christians often view church discipline from a skewed point of view. Whenever I teach 1 Corinthians 5, whether in a church or a seminary, the class members want to focus on the man's sin (v. 1) or his anticipated discipline (v. 5). Too often we try to read this passage from the point of view of the one who is about to be disciplined. And because we readily assume that an individual's freedom is the highest good, we often see church discipline as archaic, doctrinaire, and arbitrary. In a society where individual rights are highly prized and community is misunderstood or even devalued, it's easy to dissociate discipline and community. We all too quickly see the disciplined person as a victim and forget the needs of the community.

It is easy to list all kinds of reasons why church discipline is no longer appropriate. What good does it do to dismiss someone from our church when they can easily find a new church home down the block or across town? Unlike Corinth, where the church Paul had founded was undoubtedly the only one in the area, our towns and cities have many churches that would be only too willing to gain a new member, no questions asked. It makes us wonder if church discipline can possibly be taken seriously. And what about the possibility of legal action? Are we willing to defend our church's disciplinary action in a civil court if it comes to that, as it has on a number of occasions? One might even question whether church discipline is legitimate in light of the fact that all Christians are sinners. Doesn't church discipline target the most obvious of sins, especially sexual ones, while ignoring the insidious ones that truly harm the community?

Still, in spite of the commonly voiced wariness of church discipline, most Christians with whom I discuss this issue can recall several times in their communities when it would have been far better to remove the leaven than to let it poison the whole lump of dough. Almost everyone has a story of a pastor whose adulterous relationships, known but unchecked by timid congregations and incompetent denominational officials, left a wake of personal and communal destruction. Equally common are reports of illicit affairs between elders or board members. In the absence of an official judgment on the matter, the community is confused about its moral standards and becomes divided as people support or denounce the offending parties. Perhaps most of all, people tell of horrendous relational problems that have been allowed to flourish. Member A hates Member B, and vice versa. They talk openly against one another and recruit people to support their position. Congregational discussion of issues becomes impossible and worship services are poisoned. In the end entire churches are split into camps. Because a congregation is unable to treat the hatred in its early stages, the resulting conflict can go on for years, even decades.

Paul's essential message in this section of 1 Corinthians is one with which few of us can disagree: the Christian community must be protected against pollution by the world's ethical standards. The community is God's temple, chosen and holy, and therefore we should be concerned about it. It is vulnerable, as the attitude of the Corinthians and Paul's image of the leaven and the dough indicate. We have been given the daunting task of maintaining the purity of the church. Unfortunately, Paul answers few of our questions about the process we should use to preserve this purity. What sins warrant the sinner's expulsion from the church? Why doesn't Paul call for the censure of those Corinthians frequenting brothels? Although we know that the church is to gather for the excommunication of the sinner (5:4), what would actually take place at this gathering? Would the community recite their grievances against the offender or perhaps hold a service of excommunication? Would the offender be given a chance to repent? We can only speculate on these and other questions. Most denominations use the words of Jesus in Matthew 18:15–17 as their primary biblical resource on the process of church discipline.

But Paul's message is extremely helpful for us because it points out the characteristics of a Christian community that is able to discipline its members. Three things are important. The first is that the community will recognize that it needs to be shielded from invasion by the world's standards. The Christian community is both valuable and vulnerable. The modern church desperately needs to come to terms with this understanding of community. Time and time again people tell of ongoing ethical problems in their churches that are simply ignored. Two members of the church are living together outside of marriage and no one protests; a long-time member is an alcoholic and known abuser of his wife, yet the church is silent. To ignore these problems is to declare either that the community cannot be affected by such behavior, a common assumption in the modern church, or, perhaps even more ominous, that the Christian community is not something worth protecting. All too often the latter is the essential problem; the community is simply not valued enough to warrant taking on the burden and responsibility that come with an act of church discipline.

The second characteristic of a disciplining community, according to Paul, is that it will have a clear understanding of its ethical standards. The Corinthian community is strongly influenced by the morality of the Greco-Roman world. A good part of Paul's task is to help the Christians at Corinth reconstruct their ethics, to resocialize them on the basis of the Jewish law and their new relationship with Christ. Paul's condemnation of immorality and his listing of things that Christians must not do (5:11; 6:9–10) indicate that he believes there are ethical absolutes in the Christian life, even for these Gentiles. A Christian community must know and accept these norms before any discipline can take place. Too often we in the modern church fail to protect the ethical integrity of our communities because we're not quite sure how to define right and wrong. Like the Corinthians, we allow ourselves to be influenced by the world to the extent that we become ethically confused. Paul's assertion that the health of the Christian community is dependent upon its ethical boundaries is a wake-up call to a modern church that is willing to assume with the world that all is relative.

The third characteristic of a disciplining community is that it has compassion for the offending member. Paul's judgment on the man engaged in sexual immorality, severe as it sounds, is intended to lead to his salvation (5:5). The desired end of every disciplinary action in the church is remediation. The extremely unpleasant ordeal of deciding to excommunicate a fellow Christian is hard to endure unless it is motivated by a love that seeks the ultimate welfare of that person. But even the initial questioning of the behavior of a fellow member, whether it leads to formal discipline or not, must be motivated by a deep concern for the spiritual welfare of that person. It is loving families that care enough to discipline their members. I have often thought that many of the disciplinary crises churches face could have been avoided if someone in the community were loving enough to confront the offending individual early on. Informal discipline in which one member lovingly and discreetly reminds another member of her or his deviation from Christian ethical standards should be a common occurrence in the community. The painful reality in the modern church is that too often we simply don't care enough about individuals in our community to assume responsibility for helping them live the Christian life.

Church history is filled with examples of Christian communities taking discipline seriously. Basil, Bishop of Caesarea (ca. 330–379), offers what was then probably a common sentence for a man engaged in an incestuous affair. After the man repents and has given up the sinful relationship, he is allowed only to weep outside the church door for three years. For the next three years he is allowed to hear the Word preached, but is excluded from prayers. For the three years after that he is permitted to pray and weep in the church on his knees. Finally, in the tenth year, he is readmitted to membership, although he may not partake of communion for another two years![7] Think of what this pronouncement says about the sanctity of the community involved, to say nothing of Basil's authority! If discipline is an important aspect of healthy Christian community, as Paul asserts, and if it has been practiced throughout the history of the church, as this extreme example from Basil shows, then we must ask ourselves why discipline is so seldom used in the modern church. What does our omission say about how we value community and the individuals in it? What does it say about our community's ethical standards and its relationship to the world? Discipline should be an expected function of a community that has a clear sense of what it is striving to become in Christ.

Boundaries

Everything Paul says in 1 Corinthians 5–6, his instructions about church discipline, lawsuits, and personal morality, affirm that Christian community is defined over against the ethics of the world. Our ethical lives need boundaries. The word *boundaries* implies that there are places we may and may not go, things we may and may not do. Paul assumes that Christians must follow certain basic ethical standards that are quite different from those of the world. These standards not only protect the purity of the community, but they also become a bond that holds the community together. Christians live lives that are unique and demanding. They have given up their old worldly ways (6:11), and they gain a new common identity both in their relationship with Christ and in the life that flows from it. The battle scars that result from trying to maintain the ethical boundaries between church and world are an important source of the unity of the Christian community.

Where do the ethical boundaries lie in our Christian communities? Do they distinguish us from the world? Do our children have a clear sense of what these boundaries are? Do members of our communities have a common identity that grows out of the demands of living the Christian life? The difficulty we have in answering these questions shows us why we find Paul's words in chapters 5 and 6 so threatening and why many of us would like to ignore them if we could. It's hard to avoid the conclusion that often we have not feared the world as it influences the ethical practices of our communities. Like the Corinthians we need to be resocialized; we need to give up our comfortable relationship with the mores of American culture and hear again the foolish demands of the One who died on the cross. If there is just as much hate and adultery and deception and self-love in one's church as there is in the various communities the world offers, then a vital part of what distinguishes Christian community has disappeared.

If the community's purity is so important, shouldn't we attempt to isolate ourselves from the world, as many Christians have over the years? Isolation might be a proper reaction if purity were our only goal, but Paul clearly states that it is not. Christians cannot (5:10), indeed must not, avoid the world. Paul's entire ministry is built on the assumption that God's call to discipleship carries the mandate to witness in the world. The world must not enter the church, but the church must enter the world. As Paul says in Romans 12–14, Christians inhabit the world as "living sacrifice[s]" (12:1). They live in harmony with and witness to those around them (12:14–21). They pay their taxes (13:1–7) and wrestle with certain of the world's customs (chapter 14). In all of this they are not to conform to the world, but to live as people who have been transformed through the renewal that comes from God (12:2).

Our task is simple: all we need do is live the Christian life in the midst of a hostile world. But how is such a task possible? Paul talks about empowerment for the Christian life in many ways, and implicit throughout 1 Corinthians 5–6 is his belief that Christian community is an important basis for our discipleship in the world. Being part of a community that strives to be God's holy temple, that follows ethical standards that radically set it apart from world, is an important part of what enables us to enter the world undaunted. The community gives us an identity that is stronger than the one projected by the world. One of the greatest fallacies in modern Christianity is the assumption that an individual can follow the rigors of the Christian life apart from community. We need both the support and the critique a faithful community can offer. We need to be part of a community that will constantly remind us who we are in Christ.

One of the ways individualism affects American culture is in the distinction between public and private morality. Many people believe that what a person does in private, especially sexually, is that person's own business. There has been tremendous turmoil around this issue as it applies to the conduct of the former president of the United States and other elected officials. Our national discussion of sexual behavior appears to be moving us toward a new consensus that so-called private sins are not as private as we once thought, but in a politically charged environment these trends are not always easy to read. The modern church, unfortunately, has been susceptible to the individualistic way of thinking about ethics. The best proof of this is mainline denominations' extreme hesitance to use church discipline for sexual sins. Paul's words in chapters 5–6 are for many churches an unpleasant reminder that an individual Christian's ethical behavior always has consequences; it always affects the purity of the community (5:6–8). What we do in the physical body affects our relationship with Christ and by extension our relationship with all of the other community members, whose bodies are also linked with Christ (6:12–20).

All of us have known Christians who try to construct their ethical lives on the basis of the distinction between the public and the private. Often it seems to work, at least for a while. What we see, or perhaps what we choose to see, as members of their community is well-adjusted people striving to live the Christian life. But invariably the facade collapses. Paul's words are true; these so-called private sins pollute our relationship with Christ and with others in the community to the extent that at some point they can no longer be hidden. One of the saddest things in the Christian life is the humiliation of fellow Christians whose immorality has been exposed. We should mourn for people whose "private" sins have caught up with them. But we should also mourn for the community that has failed to offer clear ethical boundaries and has failed to be a nurturing and disciplining presence in the life of the individual.

These chapters in 1 Corinthians are for us what they were for the original hearers, a sobering call to rethink our relationship to the world as it affects Christian community. In part, Paul motivates us in this difficult section by telling us that the world and its influences are passing away; in the end, Christians will judge the world (6:2) and experience the kingdom of God fully (6:10). But Paul motivates us most powerfully by once again reminding us how God's future has entered our present. Every few paragraphs, in the midst of strong indictment, Paul challenges us by showing us what we already are in God's eyes and in light of what we have received in Jesus Christ. Because we as a community are already unleavened, already the recipients of the Lamb's sacrifice, we can strive to be a pure batch of dough (5:7). Because we already know what it means to be washed, sanctified, and justified through Jesus Christ and the Spirit, we are motivated to live the morally pure life (6:11). And because Christ has paid the price to redeem us out of slavery, we are free to glorify God in our bodies (6:20). The comfort we have is that God is with us in our struggle to build holy and pure communities. The Christ who saves us through the foolishness of the cross, who has been sacrificed, who has washed us and bought us with a price, is present as we seek to establish these foolish, world-denying communities.

Women and Men
in Community

1 Corinthians 7; 11:2–16

It could easily be argued that how we relate as women and men is the most fundamental community issue we face as Christians. It involves everyone. Why is it, then, that issues of sexuality and gender are so often left undiscussed in the local church, the tensions they raise allowed to smolder beneath the surface? Do we assume that how we function as men and women is genetically determined and therefore beyond our control? Or have we become so accustomed to our culture's understanding of gender that we assume traditional definitions cannot be challenged, even when they stand in conflict with the Christian message? Perhaps we avoid these issues precisely because all of us are either male or female; we fear that once the discussion is opened, we will be inescapably drawn into the fray.

Fortunately for us, Paul is not reluctant to discuss issues of sexuality and gender, even when they appear to be private or mundane matters. He knows that the questions of how marital partners relate sexually, how singleness is valued, and even how women and men dress are not without significance for Christian community. Paul most directly discusses the topic of men and women in community in two places in 1 Corinthians, in chapter 7 and in verses 2–16 of chapter 11. The specific problems he addresses in each of these passages are quite different from one another: in 1 Corinthians 7 he must deal with ascetics who believe that sexual relations must be eliminated from the Christian life; in 1 Corinthians 11:2–16 he confronts those who believe that Christianity frees them from traditional gender-related dress codes. Yet the two passages also share common ground. The barrier to community Paul must confront in these passages is a self-serving attitude about sexuality and

gender that causes division between women and men rather than bringing them together in fellowship.

1 Corinthians 7

In chapter 7 Paul finally begins to respond to issues the Corinthians
raised in their most recent letter to him. He starts by quoting the letter:
"It is well for a man not to touch a woman" (7:1). Here Paul uses the
word *touch* (*haptomai*) in a way that was common in his day and is not
unusual in modern English; it refers to sexual touching or sexual relations. Some people in the Corinthian church were asserting that Christians, even husbands and wives, should avoid sexual activity altogether.
To those of us who live in a world where sexual gratification is constantly touted as one of the highest goods, this attitude seems baffling.
But in Paul's day asceticism, the practice of denying the desires of the
body for religious or philosophical reasons, was not unusual. Both the
Greek philosophical schools of the Cynics and the Stoics and popular
religion equated sexual abstinence with spiritual power. For some, the
body was a problem; its base impulses must be subdued before a person could experience true spiritual enlightenment.

One wonders if Paul's example and words might inadvertently feed
these ascetic leanings. We know that the apostle was unmarried, and he
later describes singleness as a gift from God (7:7) and a legitimate sacrifice for ministry (9:5). More telling, however, is the language Paul uses
in baptism services. Galatians 3:27–28 is probably typical: "As many of
you as were baptized into Christ have clothed yourselves with Christ.
There is neither Jew or Greek, there is no longer slave or free, there is
no longer male and female; for you are one in Christ Jesus." If it is true,
as Paul asserts, that old religious, class, and gender barriers have been
left behind in Jesus Christ, what does that mean for our sexuality? As
people who are experiencing the power and change of the new age in
Christ, the Corinthians could easily assume that they are androgynous
creatures for whom sexual relations are no longer appropriate.

It is interesting to speculate about the makeup of this ascetic group
in the Corinthian church. One wonders if Paul is responding to a group
that is composed especially of women, just as Paul's words about sexual boundaries in chapters 5 and 6 appear to be directed especially
toward men. Notice how Paul explicitly addresses both women and men
in chapter 7 (see vv. 3–4; 10; 12–13; 32–34; and 36–40), something that
occurs only here in his letters. Certainly it is women, burdened as they
are with the dangers of childbirth and the primary responsibility for
child care, who will be most liberated by celibacy. Is it possible that two

gender-based groups with opposing views of sexuality form another one of the divisions Paul refers to in 1:10? Imagine the tension in a church containing such extremes, members of one group claiming that Christian freedom allows them to ignore sexual boundaries ("all things are lawful" [6:12]), those of another asserting that experiencing the new age in Jesus Christ demands sexual abstinence. What would have been lost on both factions is the essential similarity of their positions: both misunderstand the responsibility that comes with living as a Christian in a physical body.

Paul responds to these ascetics as he does, not because he doubts that celibacy can be a good thing, but because he disagrees both with their motivation and with their apparent claim that celibacy is something that all Christians should practice. In chapter 7 Paul addresses two groups in the church: those who are married or formerly married (vv. 2–16), and those who are contemplating marriage (vv. 25–38). Because of the possibility that a deprived partner might fall into immorality (vv. 2, 5), married couples should continue to engage in sexual relations (to "have" each other [v. 2]). The only exception to this, according to Paul, is abstinence by mutual agreement and during short periods of spiritual regeneration (v. 5). Paul wishes that all were single as he is, for reasons he will give later, but he understands that both marriage and singleness can be seen as gifts from God (v. 7).

Paul is in general agreement with the ascetics concerning the formerly married (*agamos* is best translated as "widower") except that he is less dogmatic. While singleness is preferable, widows and widowers are encouraged to remarry if they have strong sexual appetites (7:8–9). But Paul strongly disagrees with those who value celibacy to the extent that they encourage Christians to dissolve their marriages (v. 10–11). Here there is a clear command from the Lord (v. 10). The water is murkier with regard to marriages between believers and unbelievers (vv. 12–16; cf. 2 Corinthians 6:14–7:1). Paul's advice (*not* the Lord's! [v. 12]) is that women and men who are married to unbelievers should not divorce them, because unbelievers are made holy through their believing spouses (v. 14). If the unbeliever seeks divorce, so be it. Peace, apparently, takes priority over the possibility that the unbelieving spouse might be converted (vv. 15–16)!

If the ascetics' policy was to renounce sexual relations and even dissolve existing marriages, Paul's advice to the Corinthians is essentially the opposite: to remain as they are (v. 8, 11, and especially vv. 17–24). He supports this stance in the first part of chapter 7 on the basis of his understanding of the power of the sexual drive and the sanctity of marriage, but he gives a more comprehensive explanation beginning with verse 17. There he says that Christians should not be overly concerned with changing their outward circumstances, because these things have been relativized in light of the salvation they have in Jesus Christ (vv. 17–24). Paul employs his frequently used images of circumcision/uncircumcision and slave/free to illustrate how old religious and class barriers that divide human beings have become meaningless in Christ (see 12:12–13; Galatians 3:28). Circumcision/uncircumcision is a helpful example of a circumstance that Christians need not try to change, but Paul indicates in the second part of verse 21 that he believes that slavery does not fall into this category. A slave need not be concerned about his situation, Paul says, but "if you are able to gain your freedom, make use of the opportunity" (cf. the awkward translation in the NRSV). Still, Paul continues with the image because it so graphically illustrates how salvation in Christ relativizes life's circumstances, even those things we would like to change but cannot. In Christ, slaves become free and free people become slaves (v. 22). In a real sense all Christians are freed slaves, "bought with a price" (v. 23).

Paul's advice to those who are engaged to be married (virgins [v. 25]) is also "remain as you are" (v. 26), but he further clarifies the reason for saying so. It is Paul's opinion (he has no command of the Lord about this [v. 25]!) that the unmarried should remain single because of the "present necessity" (v. 26; cf. the NRSV: the "impending crisis"). This translation of the ambiguous phrase *enestōsan anangkēn* recognizes the eschatological overtones of what Paul is saying. Those who are married will experience additional distress (v. 28) in the short time before Christ's return (cf. Mark 13:17–20). In lines that are both beautiful and open to misinterpretation, Paul stresses the eschatological context of our lives by explaining how everything we do is part of a world that is passing away:

> From now on, let even those who have wives be as though they had none[!], and those who mourn as though they were not mourning, and those who rejoice as though they were not rejoicing, and those who buy as though they had no possessions, and those who deal with the world as though they had no dealings with it (vv. 29–31).

Beware, Paul seems to be saying, of attaching significance to things of this world, even good things, in a way that makes life before the return of Christ a heavier burden.

But the main thrust of this translation of *enestōsan anangkēn* lies in the necessity or obligation to do the Lord's work before the end of the age (see 9:16, where Paul uses *anangkē* to refer to the obligation he feels to preach). The phrase thus helps interpret 7:32–34 and finally gives the reader a positive reason for remaining single. While the married man or woman is necessarily concerned with his or her spouse and the things of this world (vv. 33–34), the unmarried man or woman is freed to devote himself or herself to the affairs of the Lord (vv. 32, 34). In light of the nearness of the end (vv. 29, 31) and the importance of the task (the "present necessity"), singleness is the better path, the one Paul himself has chosen (vv. 7–8). Paul recommends the unmarried life for those who have been gifted in this way (v. 7), because single people can offer "unhindered devotion to the Lord" (v. 35).

Perhaps Paul's most obvious conflict with the ascetics has to do with the nature of marriage. Unlike those he is addressing, Paul affirms the sanctity of marriage and, more important, knows that there is an indissoluble link between believers' marriages and the Christian communities in which they operate. Paul's conflict here is the opposite side of the issue discussed in chapters 5 and 6 of the epistle. In that situation a violation of the marriage vow in the form of immorality leads to pollution of the entire community (5:1–6). Here a rejection of sexuality by some married people increases the possibility of immoral behavior among their spouses (7:2) and even calls into question the value of marriage itself (v. 10). Paul envisions a Christian community in which a man and a woman realize that their marriage affects other marriages, affects the ethical standards of the community, and even affects outsiders' perception of the community.

Paul also disagrees with the ascetics in the Corinthian church concerning the power and purpose of sex. Unlike the ascetics, Paul realizes that sexual passion is something that cannot be ignored. Couples must not withhold sex from one another (7:1–6), and singles and the previously married must be honest about their sexuality as they contemplate marriage (vv. 9, 36). Human beings have bodies; they are sexual creatures. And they are unavoidably male or female. For Paul, sex within marriage is a natural and good way for women and men to be in relationship with one another. If the Christian ascetics are like other ascetics of their day, they abstain from sex in order that they might attain individual spiritual power or enlightenment. The physical body stands in the way of religious fulfillment. One wonders whether the ascetics at Corinth view themselves as androgynous beings—such a view is a natural consequence of this perception of the body. If so, they are polar opposites of Paul: he sees humanity as two distinct sexes moving toward relationships; they see people as identical androgynous beings moving toward individual spiritual improvement. In light of the evidence here and throughout the letter (see chapters 5, 6, and 15) that the Corinthians have a low view of the body, one wonders how receptive they would be to Paul's metaphor of the Christian community as body (10:17; 11:29; 12:12–27).

The paradox of Paul's words in chapter 7 is that he both emphasizes the importance of the Corinthians' current situation in life (whether they are married or single) and relativizes it by stressing who they are in Jesus Christ (vv. 19, 22–23) and the nature of their eschatological task (vv. 26, 29–34). The ascetics were apparently making their decision about sexuality the center of their religious life. For Paul, how we function as men and women is very important, but it must not be confused with what is ultimately important, the inbreaking of the new age God has inaugurated in Jesus Christ. One wonders how the ascetics at Corinth would have heard his exhortation to "let even those who have wives be as though they had none" (v. 29). The words could easily be interpreted to *support* their position! And yet Paul's words do critique the ascetics in a significant way, if understood correctly. One's sexual identity is not the ultimate touchstone in the Christian life. Paul is reminding the members of the church at Corinth that who they are as Christian men and women grows out of the eschatological salvation they have in Christ, not vice versa.

In the process of speaking about the place of sexuality in the Christian life, Paul does a truly amazing thing; he treats men and women as equals. As we have seen, the basis for this equality is certainly not an androgynous, body-denying view of women and men. Rather, Paul's vision of community grows out of his understanding that the gospel message challenges culture's understanding of gender roles, especially the roles of women. What exactly does it mean that for the Christian there is "no longer male and female" (Galatians 3:28)?

Paul challenges two aspects of first-century views of gender roles. In 7:1–5 Paul clearly states that sexual mutuality is an important part of Christian marriage. Not just husbands, but wives also have recognized conjugal rights (v. 3). To the widely accepted view that husbands have authority over their wives' bodies, Paul boldly adds that a husband's body is under the authority of his wife (v. 4)! Even short periods of abstinence must be agreed upon by both partners (v. 5). Of course, Paul's response here is directed toward only one aspect of the marital relationship. But considering the importance he attaches to sexuality in marriage, it is hard to believe that Paul would not affirm mutuality in other areas of married life as well. And certainly how men and women relate to one another within marriage will have a significant impact upon how the genders relate in the larger Christian community.

The second area in which Paul is at odds with traditional gender roles is his support for singleness, including that of women. Biblical accounts of the plight of the barren women (Sarah, Hannah, Elizabeth) reflect attitudes that were widely accepted in Paul's day even in the non-Jewish world; to be fulfilled, a woman must marry and bear children. Perhaps the best New Testament example of this attitude is the statement in 1 Timothy 2:15 that a woman "will be saved through childbearing." (Could Paul possibly be the author of these words?) In the Roman Empire there were even laws mandating marriage, and remarriage for divorcées and widows, as means of protecting traditional family values and ensuring a high birth rate.[1]

Now Paul is saying that it is acceptable, even preferable, for ordinary women—and men—to remain single and serve the Lord. He gives women options they did not have before. They are free to follow God's calling, free from the responsibilities that come with marriage. The fact that singleness is common in the modern church must not blind us to the fact that Paul's support for the single life is extraordinary in the first century. Men and women are equally invited to participate in the ministry of the church. The tasks of the Christian community will be taken up by people of both genders. Paul's care in addressing both men and women in chapter 7 affirms this equality (vv. 2–5; 10–11; 12–16; 32–34). Here there is no trace of the traditional household code and its sometimes patriarchal restrictions (cf. 1, 2 Timothy, Colossians 3:18–4:1; Ephesians 5:21–6:9). Paul is taking great pains to show the Corinthians that Christian community, in stark contrast to the world, equally values the gifts of women and men.

One wonders how effective Paul's appeal, especially his assertion that they should "remain as they are," is in convincing the ascetics. They know that Paul's preaching had already turned things upside-down in their Christian community. Paul is in the awkward position of both preaching a gospel that advocates radical change and monitoring the Corinthians for change that is inappropriate or goes too far. What would be appealing to the ascetics is his strong affirmation of the equality of women and men, both in marriage and in the ministry of the church. For the larger Corinthian church, Paul's response provides clear alternatives to the ascetics' stance, especially in terms of what it means to be a Christian community. Christians are unavoidably sexual beings, male and female, and sexuality in marriage is one important way for men and women to be in relationship. Christian marriage, both in terms of how men and women relate and how ethical boundaries are defined, always affects Christian community. Singleness is a good alternative to marriage for those who are called to it, not because it brings some kind of individual spiritual empowerment, but because it allows women and men to be about the "affairs of the Lord" (7:32) in urgent times (7:26). In the end, any attempt to give one's sexual status ultimate importance is doomed to failure; what distinguishes us as married or unmarried people is relativized in light of the inbreaking power of the gospel message (7:29–31).

1 Corinthians 11:2–16

Paul's obscure and seemingly patriarchal arguments in 1 Corinthians 11:2–16 surely make this one of the most avoided passages in the New Testament. This is unfortunate, because the passage does contain helpful insights about men and women in Christian community. At first glance the behavior with which Paul is concerned seems innocuous enough: certain women in the Corinthian church are ignoring society's dress codes. More specifically, these women are participating in communal worship with their heads "uncovered" (v. 5). This might mean, as has traditionally been assumed, that they are without a veil (see the NRSV). But Paul never uses the word *veil* in this passage, and veiling is not a common thing for Hellenistic women of the first century. In light of Paul's argument that a woman's hair "is given to her for a covering" (v. 15) and his repeated mention of appropriate hairstyles (vv. 5–6, 14–15), it is perhaps better to think of this uncovered state simply as one in which a woman's hair is not bound up in the customary manner but is allowed to fall down over her shoulders naturally.

What is at stake here? It has often been speculated that Paul is especially concerned with the church's external image, lest the Corinthians' non-Christian neighbors get a false impression of what happens at Christian worship. We know that unbound hair is often associated with either prostitutes or pagan prophetesses and their ecstatic behavior during worship. Under the leadership of these Corinthian women, do people fail to worship "decently and in order" (14:40)? We can only guess, but it may be that the apostle is fearful that the church's potential for outreach, always a prime concern, is being compromised.

Still, this explanation remains speculative because Paul does not mention these concerns in his letter. Nor does he write as though this is primarily a matter of abuse of personal freedom. He does not repeat his mantra that "'all things are lawful,' . . . but not all things are beneficial" (6:12; 10:23), although those who dislike Paul's convoluted arguments in this passage might wish he had. Instead, Paul's approach is to address these challenges to traditional coiffure in terms of gender identity and the relationship between the sexes. Men and women are different, he argues, and must wear their hair differently from one another and in a way that is consistent with society's gender expectations (11:3, 7–9, 14–15). Those who reject such traditional gender markers shame the other sex and their own (vv. 5–6, 14–15).

This means that Paul understands the head-covering issue to be a threat to the Corinthian community in a way that is very similar to the way the threat he deals with in chapter 7 is. Does he assume that the same women are involved in both cases? The apostle's argument shows that he fears these women are seeking to be liberated altogether from any uniqueness associated with being female. Perhaps they are convinced that their new, spirit-filled life in the Christian faith should allow them to rise above their sexuality. If there is no male and female in Christ, should not all dress distinctions between the genders be eliminated? It is also possible that this rejection of gender distinctions by the Corinthian women was fueled by the patriarchy of their society and even their church. The abandonment of traditional hairstyles would be a protest against the ways in which women were marked as the inferior gender. Because women and men are one in Christ, it would seem reasonable to challenge all the old ways in which society has discriminated against women in its attempt to divide the genders.

What we might see initially as either a minor incident about dress or a legitimate protest against traditional hairstyles, Paul views as a serious problem concerning gender identity. It is a threat to community, perhaps in terms of how the church is perceived by non-Christians, but certainly in terms of how men and women relate within the community, how the genders function, and how the identity of one gender affects the other. As was the case in chapter 7, Paul is caught in the dilemma of both advocating a radical new freedom in Jesus Christ and cautioning against certain expressions of freedom he deems illegitimate. His strategy in 11:2–16 reflects the tension; Paul argues that even for Christians there are ongoing differences between men and women (vv. 3–10, 13–16), but he also stresses that in the Lord there is a wonderful new interdependence and equality between the genders (vv. 11–12).

The first of Paul's arguments in support of the differences between men and women revolves around shame—how the dress of these women at Corinth is disgraceful to themselves and especially to the men of the community (vv. 3–6). Paul assumes that one's culture defines what is acceptable in terms of appearance; any person who radically departs from the norm will be shamed. According to Paul, the disgrace these Corinthian women bring on themselves and their fellow Christians by having their heads "uncovered" during worship is similar to the shame that would result if they were to cut their hair short or shave their heads (vv. 5–6).

Inappropriate dress and the shame it produces are most clearly linked to the uniqueness of each of the genders in the theological rationale Paul offers in verses 3–5. It is here, of course, that the apostle's argument becomes problematic for many modern readers. Paul posits a God-Christ-man-woman hierarchy (v. 3) and argues that a disregard for traditional hairstyles brings shame to a man or woman's "head" (*kephalē*), the person who precedes him or her in the hierarchy (vv. 4–5). Men who pray or prophesy with an unacceptable coiffure disgrace their "head," Christ. Women who pray or prophesy with their hair unbound disgrace their "head," the men in the community. It is important to note that Paul is not simply speaking about husbands and wives here, although the words *anēr* and *gynē* can be translated that way (see the NRSV, v. 3). Both the first-century use of the metaphor "head" and Paul's argument based on creation in verses 7–9 suggest that he intends the word to mean "source" rather than "ruler." Man is the source of woman in the sense that she was created from him, as we read in Genesis chapter 2. Christ, as an agent of creation, is the source of every man, while God is the source of Christ in the incarnation. This translation of the word *head* certainly does not eliminate all the patriarchal implications of Paul's argument, but it does explain how his words remind the Corinthians that the differences between men and women go back to creation itself.

Paul's next argument (vv. 7–9), no less problematic for modern readers, is a further explanation of how women and men are different on the basis of creation. Undergirded by the second creation account and its assertion that the male was created first and the female created from him and for him (Genesis 2:4–25; 1 Corinthians 11:8–9), Paul argues that women and men must cover their heads in different ways because they reflect different beings: men are the image and glory of God, while women are the glory of men (v. 7; the NRSV translates *doxa*, "glory," as "reflection"). What Paul fails to mention is that Genesis 1:26–27 says that *both* genders are created in God's image. Because Paul gives no explanation of what he means by "glory," a word not used in the creation accounts, we are left wondering why only men are the glory of God and in what sense women are the glory of men. It is clear that Paul wants to distinguish between the genders, but the way he does so in his embellished treatment of the creation account makes it appear that he also wants to affirm that men are superior.

Verse 10, which appears to be a conclusion to the argument in verses 3–9, may well be the most opaque sentence Paul ever wrote. The variety of English translations indicates just how unsure we are about Paul's intended meaning. We expect him to say that women ought to have their heads covered (in contrast to v. 7, where men "ought not"), but what Paul literally says is, "For this reason a woman ought to have authority (*exousia*) over her head, because of the angels." In light of what Paul has just finished arguing, it hardly seems possible that he is now declaring a woman's freedom to make her own choice regarding hairstyle. It is more likely that a woman's "authority over her head" simply refers to her responsibility to control her hair and wear it up, but this interpretation is also speculative.[2] Equally mysterious is Paul's assertion that women should exercise this authority "because of the angels." Does he actually think that angels might lust after women who wear their hair in an alluring, unbound manner (see Genesis 6:1–4)? Or, more probably, is he saying that women must conduct themselves properly at worship because angels are thought to be present there? Hopefully Paul's lack of explanation for his terse remarks in verse 10 indicates that his Corinthian audience knew what he was talking about, even though we may no longer be able to.

At this point in the passage we modern readers might be tempted to give up in frustration, not only because of what seems to us an incredible lack of clarity, but especially because of the patriarchal arguments Paul employs here. The apostle appears to be trying to put the women of Corinth in their place. His theologizing here *is* patriarchal and needs to be recognized as such. Taken by themselves, Paul's arguments in verses 3–10 affirm a hierarchy in which men come first and the genders appear to relate to God differently. This is very unfortunate, not only because such patriarchal statements are inconsistent with what we see in the rest of his correspondence, but more important, because they do not lie at the heart of what Paul is hoping to communicate to the Corinthians.

Paul's purpose in verses 3–10 is not to persuade the Corinthians that men are superior, but that men and women are different and must therefore dress differently. He does not attempt to show that the men of the community have authority over the women. He does not call upon the men to initiate disciplinary action against these women. Instead, using terms of shame and glory, he reminds the women that their dress affects their unique relationship with men. And notice how Paul rejects the priority of men in an important area of corporate life by assuming that women, too, function as leaders during worship. In carefully balanced clauses (vv. 4–5) Paul affirms a radically inclusive policy: both genders pray and prophesy when the community gathers. Prayer, of course, can be private, but prophesying, as Paul defines the activity, refers to the delivery of proclamations during corporate worship (14:3–5, 22–25). Paul's theological attempts to convince certain Corinthian women of the uniqueness of their gender shows just how difficult it can be to argue that women and men are different without also giving the impression that one gender is superior to the other.

The best indication that Paul has not been arguing for the subordination of women comes in verses 11–12, where he strongly affirms the interdependence and equality of Christian women and men: "Nevertheless, in the Lord woman is not independent of man or man independent of woman. For just as woman came from man, so man comes through woman; but all things come from God." The dramatic shift represented by these verses probably does not mean Paul has come to his senses and is retracting his former arguments. Much more likely, Paul realizes that his theologizing in verses 3–5 and 7–9 could easily be read in a patriarchal way and that he must clarify his intentions.

In the Lord, Paul says, women and men are not "independent" (*chōris*) of one another; he is clearly responding to the possible implications of his own words (and perhaps especially those in v. 9): that women are responsible to men but not vice versa. Some scholars have suggested that *chōris* might be better translated "different"; men and women are not different from one another.[3] But the whole point of Paul's argument in verses 3–9 is to show that the genders are different! Much more likely, Paul is saying literally that women and men are "not without" one another.[4] Neither gender is complete without the other. Paul is not saying, of course, that people must be married in order to achieve wholeness. Rather, he is affirming the mutual dependence of all men and women in Christian community. And because all things come from God and because women give birth to men (v. 12), any argument for the priority and superiority of men based on the creation accounts is meaningless (he is responding to the possible implications of his own words in vv. 3 and 7). Without relinquishing his opinion that women and men are different, Paul now asserts that our common origin in God also gives the genders an equality that is perhaps best illuminated in this passage by Paul's assumptions about shared leadership during worship (vv. 4–5).

Paul concludes his arguments in verses 2–16 by moving away from his theological arguments and inviting the Corinthians to agree ("judge for yourselves" [v. 13]) with his final comments on the subject (vv. 13–16). Nature (meaning here "social custom") teaches that women and men must be differentiated by the way they wear their hair. Those who deviate from social custom are dishonored (v. 14; cf. vv. 4–6); those who accept it are honored (v. 15). Finally, Paul appeals to the larger Christian community and to the apparent consensus on this particular matter. The Christians at Corinth who are "contentious" about issues of coiffure need to be reminded how out of step they are with the wider church.

This passage is certainly problematic. Instead of a clear and comprehensive statement about how Christian women and men relate, we get a series of unanswered questions. Why does Paul use such obscure theological arguments in verses 3–5 and 7–9, especially when they are so open to misinterpretation? What exactly does he mean when he says that men are the head of women, that women are the glory of men, that women's behavior shames men, or that angels are somehow involved in all of this? Exactly why have the women been avoiding traditional hairstyles in the first place, and why does Paul say so little about their motivation for taking this radical step? We need to remind ourselves that Paul is not writing to us. His words are one half of a conversation about a specific issue in the Corinthian church. More than is true for most passages in his letters, we remain outsiders looking in.

And yet it is also true that there is enough clarity in this passage to make it an important point of reference for our understanding of men and women in community. Paul clearly affirms ongoing differences between the genders, especially those having to do with external appearance. He is not about to agree that all traditional gender markers have been erased by the new revelation in Jesus Christ. Although we might be unsure what the apostle means when he says that the women's behavior shames or fails to properly give glory to the men, it is obvious that Paul believes that failure to observe gender differences affects how men and women relate. Most important, Paul is not comfortable with interpretations that equate distinctions between the genders with male superiority. The fact that Paul recognizes the sexist quality of his own words and makes a clear statement about the interdependence and equality of the genders (vv. 11–12) even though it might play into the hands of the women with whom he is arguing shows us just how unwilling he is to accept old patriarchal answers to the problem at Corinth. Just as significant is the apostle's affirmation of leadership roles for women during worship (v. 5). Paul envisions a Christian community in which the genders are distinct but equal, men and women value their relationship with one another, and the gifts of both genders are important.

Paul's Words for the Contemporary Community

I have often felt that what happens at the typical Midwestern potluck dinner is an excellent illustration of how genders relate in our society. If your potlucks are like the ones I attend, it is the women who invariably do most of the preparing and serving of the food. There is a traditional division of labor that presumes that food preparation is women's work and, if you probe a little deeper, that men are above such menial tasks. And what happens after the food is served? Usually the women eat with other women and the men with other men. Same-sex conversations and friendships are the rule. American society fosters narrow, sometimes rigid definitions of what men and women are supposed to do and how they are to associate with one another. Of course it needs to be said that not all traditions about women or men's work need to be challenged, nor should we try to eliminate same-sex friendships. But the potluck is a graphic example of two gender-related issues that often become barriers to community in the modern church: (1) stereotypes about the differences between men and women that commonly demean women's gifts and deprive the community of their full participation, and

(2) a caste-like separation of the genders that makes healthy relation-ships between men and women difficult.

Between Venus and Mars

A good part of the interpretive tension we feel in our passages from 1 Corinthians stems from Paul's eschatological stance. Should we lis-ten primarily to his attempts to convince the Corinthians that they are still members of this age? Or should we be especially attuned to Paul's assertion, with which the Corinthians agree, that the inbreaking of the new age has already redefined gender roles? Is Paul's message for us about gender distinctions, or is it about the equality of women and men? The difficult thing, of course, is to acknowledge that these are not alter-natives from which we can choose. Paul makes it clear that Christians are expected to live with one foot in each age.

What this means, first of all, is that the differences between men and women will continue to be an issue in Christian community. Paul is pri-marily concerned with two aspects of these differences as he writes to the Corinthians. In chapter 7 he reminds his readers that they are still sexual creatures. We cannot simply ignore the physical differences between women and men and the sexual attraction they feel for one another. Sexuality is properly expressed in marriages (7:1–5) that serve to build Christian community; it destroys community when it becomes a selfish passion that ignores boundaries and pollutes the entire church body (7:2; chapters 5–6). In chapter 11 Paul is concerned with gender differences in dress or appearance. It is not accurate to interpret Paul's words here simply as a concession to what is fashionable or politically correct. The Corinthian women's dress at worship was a radical state-ment that threatened community by shaming the men (11:5–6) and by allowing the world to misinterpret what was going on in the house churches. Paul is not telling us, as I have sometimes heard people say when they try to update this passage, that men should wear coats and ties to church and that women should wear dresses. The issue here is the extreme denial of gender differences that puts the community at risk; it is an issue that we rarely, if ever, see in the churches most of us attend.

Perhaps because of the difference between the Corinthians' situation and ours, Paul's advice about gender distinctions as they relate to sex-uality and dress, although not unimportant, seems rather obvious. The modern reader can get the impression from reading Paul that our gen-der differences are a burden that grows out of our eschatological situ-ation. Husbands and wives continue to have sexual relations, but singleness for both women and men and the ministry singleness allows are really preferable (7:32–38); society may oblige men and women to dress in certain ways, but these distinctions are petty when compared to our equality in Christ (11:11–12). This perception arises because in Paul's desire to focus on the specific issues confronting the Corinthians, he fails to move beyond gender differences as an obligation and to give a fuller picture of the unique gifts women and men bring to the community. Paul has little to say about that which is our primary concern: how the differences between women and men become a positive thing.

The focus and brevity of these passages must not blind us to the ways in which Paul does lay the foundation for Christian community that values the unique gifts of each gender. Paul affirms, of course, that the differences between women and men go back to creation itself (11:3, 7–9). And in a pivotal discussion of the function of community in chapter twelve, Paul argues that the church, like a body, must use and value its different parts if it is to operate properly (12:14–26). In that theological context Paul would certainly affirm the essential differences between men and women as gifts the community needs in order to survive. He implies this very thing in 11:11. To say that men and women are "not without" one another or are "not independent" of one another is to acknowledge that each of the genders, and hence the community, needs what the other brings to the mix.

It is certainly legitimate for the modern church to build on Paul's writings and the larger biblical witness in its concern for ways in which men and women are different. In addition to the unique gifts women and men bring, each gender has unique needs to which the community must be open. Still, there are reasons for being wary when tasks in the church are assigned on the basis of gender differences. For one thing, it is hard to determine exactly how men and women are different. Should we as Christians put any stock in popular books such as John Gray's *Men Are from Mars, Women Are from Venus*,[5] which proclaims that communication with members of the opposite sex is akin to interplanetary travel? And what about more scientific studies? Mary Field Belenky, for instance, says that women are especially adept at what she calls "connected knowing," learning that occurs through empathy and relationships, while men seem to be especially skilled at "separate knowing," a more analytical, objective way of grasping the issues.[6] In her book about the conversational styles of men and women, Deborah Tannen argues that men favor "report talk," conversation that imparts information and displays the knowledge of the speaker, while women use "rapport talk," conversation that seeks relationship.[7] Do these volumes represent a long-term consensus about the differences between the genders that we can profitably use in the church?

But there is an even more important reason for caution. Our culture is fascinated by what is different about men and women, and in a patriarchal society such as ours, to say that women are different invariably means that women are inferior. Even Paul's own theological arguments in 11:2–16 show how easy it is to fall victim to patriarchal reasoning when discussing gender differences. The church's easy capitulation to patriarchal understandings of gender differences lies at the heart of one of our most serious barriers to community. Men are stereotyped as those who have gifts in the administration, finance, and leadership of the church. Women's gifts, too often, are either left unexplored or are defined in terms of important but low-status tasks in the church, especially those that cluster around food, children, and family. A patriarchal reading of gender differences is a threat to Christian community because it assumes that women's gifts are less important than men's and hence that it is acceptable for the body to operate without an eye or hand or leg. There is an arrogant wastefulness about patriarchal communities. When women's gifts are denied, some in the community are less loved, less taught, and less prepared for ministry than they might otherwise be.

As with many important issues that affect community, answers about how men and women are different will probably come to us over the long haul. We must be both open to and critical of scientific studies on the subject. We must be wary of letting the church create gender stereotypes that fail to recognize the unusual gifts of individual women and men. We must be willing to celebrate created differences between men and women in our communities even as we live with the ambiguity of being unable to precisely define them.[8] Most important, we must employ what we learn about gender differences in a way that is consistent with the equality we have in Jesus Christ. As Paul makes clear, these differences do not divide the genders into powerful and powerless groups. Christian men and women participate in community with a strong sense of their own worth and with an appreciation of what the opposite gender will bring.

If the implications of what Paul says about gender distinctions remain ambiguous, then perhaps the message contemporary Christian communities most need to hear is the one that Paul communicates most clearly, that of the equality of women and men. This message is both surprising and radical, surprising because it does little to enhance his argument (his Corinthian "opponents" are already convinced that it is wise to leave gender differences behind), radical because it stands in sharp contrast to his patriarchal world. Paul assumes that the impact of the new age has already changed our understanding of women and men in community. "The present form of this world is passing away" (7:31); there is no going back to the status quo.

Without intending to make a comprehensive statement on the subject, Paul asserts that men and women are equal in terms of the tasks of worship leadership (11:4–5) and mission (7:32–34), in terms of authority in marital relationships (7:2–5), and in terms of their value as created beings (11:11–12). Paul assumes that there is a "functional equality"[9] between women and men in Christian community. This is important to recognize, because it has often been asserted that the equality Paul writes about occurs only at a spiritual level. There may no longer be "male and female" (Galatians 3:28), some would say, but this is a statement about our status as children of God that has nothing to do with responsibilities and relationships in the everyday life of the church. But our passages in 1 Corinthians form a commentary on the third pair in Galatians 3:28 that clearly challenges such a narrow view of gender equality. Just as the gospel radically changes what it means to relate as Jew and Greek or slave and free, so also, Paul tells us, men and women are now equal in terms of the function of the community. Men and women may have unique gifts and responsibilities, but they also have many of the *same* gifts and responsibilities.

Paul's message about the equality of men and women is the one we in mainstream churches most need to hear because it reminds us of the freedom we have as Christians to challenge society's definition of gender roles. We cannot ignore the fact that women and men have been given "sexed bodies," as Miroslav Volf puts it. Nor can we afford to be blind to challenges to gender roles that do nothing to build community (the issue in 11:2–16). But often our focus on gender differences is simply the path of least resistance, a bow to the patriarchy of our society. Paul's surprising and radical words really do force us to think again about what it means to have one foot in the new age begun in Christ. The gospel has affected this first-century man to the extent that he cannot avoid making countercultural statements. What we in the modern church most need to hear is not what Paul says to the Corinthians to tone down their eschatological zeal, but what he says, in spite of himself, about the radical new equality of women and men in Jesus Christ. We need to hear, again in the words of Miroslav Volf, that although our "sexed bodies" are still with us, the "culturally coded norms attached to sexed bodies" have been "erased in Christ."[10]

How would this functional equality affect Christian community? It would mean awareness in our communities that our stance on gender relations puts us at odds with the world. More important, the freedom to use the gifts of ministry and leadership found in both genders would more fully empower the community in its task. No longer would the gifts of half the community be underused. Women as well as men would be unhesitatingly called to serve as pastors and teachers, board members and church executives. It is hard to imagine what the church might accomplish if the joys and burdens of Christian service were equally shared by both genders.

Can We Just Be Friends?

I sometimes ask my students what their Christian communities would be like if the women of the church, fed up with being treated as if they were members of a lower caste, left to form communities of their own. What if they, like Thelma and Louise in the movie by the same name, not only questioned their assigned roles as women but also realized they could never go back to the status quo? Imagining such a situation is helpful for many reasons, not least because it reminds us of women's willingness to take on thankless jobs in the church. But in terms of personal relationships, many communities might experience only a slight impact. They would continue to be what they had always been—two communities, one composed of women and one of men.

If Christian community is threatened when it fails to use the unique and common gifts of both genders, it is also threatened when women and men are divided into two separate social groups. The genders are different in important ways, and Christian community must affirm same-sex friendships. The problem arises when women and men are categorized in such a way that friendship with someone of the other sex other than one's spouse is virtually impossible. It is assumed that certain concerns and conversation topics are the exclusive domain of a particular gender. And almost always the separation of the genders in the church is fueled by the suspicion that any relationship between a man and a woman must be of a sexual nature.

Are intergender friendships within a Christian community legitimate? And if so, what is the precise nature of these Christian relationships?[11] Paul does not directly address these issues in 1 Corinthians. Here, as in his other letters, Paul's primary concern as it relates to the bond between individual women and men is marriage and its desecration (1 Corinthians 5; 6:12–20; 7:1–16, 25–25; 2 Corinthians 6:14–7:1; 1 Thessalonians 4:1–8; cf. Ephesians 5:21–33; Colossians 3:18–19). Still, Paul's words in our 1 Corinthians passages do have important implications for the possibility and nature of relationships between Christian men and women who are not married to each other.

It is easy to overlook the fact that Christian marriage itself creates the possibility of intergender friendships. Paul, of course, has a high view of marriage. Marriages are not to be dissolved easily (7:10–16), and sexual relations take place within marriage (7:2–5) and not apart from it (5:1–12; 6:12–20). Paul's discussion of these topics with the Corinthians indicates that he believes marriage is a community issue. The marriage vows that a man and woman make are not just to one another but also to and with a larger group of Christians. Christian community protects this covenant by providing an environment in which all agree on the importance and nature of marriage, including the place of sexuality, and in which discipline for those who deviate is a real possibility (5:1–12).

Such an environment makes intergender friendships possible because they will not threaten marriages. Neither member of a couple is jealous when the other has an intergender friendship because they are both secure in their relationship and convinced of the exclusivity of their marriage bed. The community provides a safe, public setting for the intergender relationship and does not assume infidelity. As Caroline Simon says:

> A community formed around such commitments would be a safe place for marriage, family, and friendship, without segregating the sexes. Men and women would be friends both inside and outside of marriage, without trying to be asexual; friendships between men and women could be healthy and unproblematic without the friends pretending to be genderless. In such a world sexuality would not set up picket lines because sexuality and mistrust would not frequently go hand in hand.[12]

If what Paul says about marriage helps us understand how intergender friendships may be possible, what he says about the common task of Christian men and women reminds us of their inevitability. On the basis of Paul's words, I envision community in which women and men are standing shoulder to shoulder, engaged in ministry. I imagine a community in which both genders take part in worship leadership (11:4–5). Even more interesting, I imagine a community with a large group of single or formerly married men and women who are actively engaged in mission (7:32–38). Paul regularly mentions women with whom he has labored in ministry. Euodia and Syntyche are called "co-workers" who "struggled beside me in the work of the gospel" (Philippians 4:2–3). Prisca, who with her husband Aquila is leader of a house church in Corinth (1 Corinthians 16:19), is also a co-worker (Romans 16:3). Phoebe is called a deacon and benefactor of the church (Romans 16:1–2); Junia is considered to be an apostle (Romans 16:7); Mary, Tryphaena, and Tryphosa are described as important workers in their communities (Romans 16:6, 12). Is it possible that in such an environment, among those who work together in ministry, intergender friendships would not occur?

Of course this goes far deeper than simple proximity at work. Paul is clearly telling us that the task of ministry is so important that it relativizes the barriers that keep men and women apart. There is a common call to the mission of the church that makes the world's understanding of gender differences seem trite. We are still women and men, but we are also peers in ministry. And Paul emphasizes to the extreme the importance of mission by putting it into an eschatological context. The "present necessity" (1 Corinthians 7:26) gives the Corinthians' lives an urgency and focus that challenges old assumptions about relationships; it is not unlike what happens in the foxholes and on the munitions lines of an all-out war.

Having one foot in the new age forces us to rethink gender relations even apart from the issue of our common task. What do the Corinthians hear in Paul's admonition to "let even those who have wives be as though they had none . . . for the present form of this world is passing away" (7:29–31)? Clearly Paul does not intend them to give up their marriages (or their mourning or rejoicing or possessions or dealings with the world). Hopefully they hear in Paul's words a call to be freed from the pettiness that too often governs life. To experience the immanence of the new age in Jesus Christ is to be freed from the pressure to place ultimate value on things that are clearly of secondary importance. For Christians, one of the things that is "passing away" is the arbitrary barrier that separates the genders. In Christian community, having one foot in the new age means that the world's divisive labels are being challenged. There is no circumcision or uncircumcision (7:17–20), no slave or free (7:21–24), and now, at least in terms of the possibility of relationships based on Christian love, no male and female.

Although Paul does not explore the nature of intergender friendships, it is obvious that they would be governed by the same concept of love that determines all community relationships, the "more excellent way" (12:31) so eloquently described in 1 Corinthians 13. This is important to understand, because it is the best rejoinder to those who would caution against intergender friendships on the basis of Paul's warnings to the Corinthians in the passages we have been studying. We need to hear Paul's reality check. We are still "sexed beings" (7:2–5, 9, and so on), and there is certainly the possibility of sexual attraction in intergender friendships. Christian marriage is an inviolable and high-maintenance relationship (7:2–16), and friendship must not compromise it in any way.

Men and women continue to be different in significant ways (11:2–9), and friendship with someone so unlike us may not be easy, but it seems to me that intergender friendship based on Christian love can overcome these obstacles. Our love for one another grows out of the love we experience in God's act of redemption in Jesus Christ. It is modeled on his sacrifice and self-giving in the cross (see especially Philippians 2:1–11). To love in Christian community and in intergender friendships means that we seek the good of other people. Love is "patient" and "kind," "it does not insist on its own way," it "rejoices in the truth" and "bears" and "endures all things" (13:4–7). As Paul says when he encourages the Philippians to love one another on the basis of Christ's sacrificial love: "Let each of you look not to your own interests, but to the interests of others" (Philippians 2:4).

This does not mean Christian love is devoid of self-interest; our own relational needs are important. But it does mean that we do not take from other people in ways that compromise their faith, their other relationships, or their place in the Christian community. In intergender friendships based upon Christian love, each friend realizes there are limits to possession of the other person. If one or both of the friends is married, it will be understood that the friendship must never become an obstacle to that primary relationship. If it does, out of jealousy or misunderstanding, a loving friend will realize that the friendship must be sacrificed. Christian intergender friends are not naive about the differences between women and men, including the ones that can make them sexually attractive to one another, but they also understand the proper place of sexuality. On the basis of Christian love, and therefore with concern for the integrity of the other within a community that has well-defined boundaries, Christian intergender friends practice what Caroline Simon calls "innocent intimacy."[13]

Our brief discussion here addresses fully neither the complexities of these friendships nor their dangers. We must not downplay the risks involved in intergender friendships, but Paul's words do remind us of their legitimate place in Christian community. If friendships between women and men are going to occur anywhere, they should occur in the church. It is hard to imagine another situation where we would so readily condone such an obvious bifurcation of Christian community. Christian community, with its clear definition of marriage, its understanding of the genders' common call and of the urgency of the task, and especially its understanding of self-giving love, should be the place where barriers between the genders begin to be demolished.

Starting at Home

Is there a link between how men and women relate in marriage and how Christian community functions? Paul asserts that there is. He makes it clear in chapters 5 and 6 that adulterous relationships pollute the entire community. But he also believes, I would contend, that how husbands and wives treat one another in marriage will affect how men and women relate to one another in community. First Corinthians 7:2–5 is a remarkable passage because it assumes mutual power and control in marriage. If such mutuality were practiced in marriage, would it not affect how the genders relate generally in Christian community? Would a man treat his wife as a full partner in marriage, but somehow treat other women in his church as second-class citizens? Or is it likely that a woman and man would share power equally in the worship and mission of the church but feel comfortable with patriarchal understandings of marriage?

In Barbara Kingsolver's novel *The Poisonwood Bible*, there is a graphic example of this link between the marital and the communal. Reverend Nathan Price, the lead male character, is a caricature of the blundering missionary. He neglects the safety of his wife and four daughters as he accepts an assignment in the Belgian Congo shortly before the 1959 revolution. He assumes his missionary task should occupy him fully, and he gives his wife, Orleanna, the entire burden of caring for the family in a strange land. Her physical and emotional needs are simply unimportant. Reverend Price treats his wife and daughters as inferior beings, like servants who are at times useful but who certainly are not peers in ministry. Thinking back on what she and her daughters endured before they fled the Congo, and at least partly blaming herself for the ordeal, Orleanna says:

> I was his instrument, his animal. Nothing more. How we wives and mothers do perish at the hands of our own righteousness. I was just one more of those women who clamp their mouths shut and wave the flag as their nation rolls off to conquer another in war. Guilty or innocent, they have everything to lose. They *are* what there is to lose. A wife is the earth itself, changing hands, bearing scars.[14]

Nathan Price's treatment of his wife and daughters has an obvious relationship to how he pastors in this African community. He is callous and condescending toward those women who try their best to help him and his family. His first words to the community are a harangue about the attire of the very women who are serving him during their welcome feast. He treats the men of the community as ignorant and inferior as well. He ignores traditions and structures of power. He grows indignant with anyone who tries to argue with him. Price is so obsessed with his own mission and status that he refuses to listen when chief Tata Ndu asserts that the river, filled with crocodiles, is not a good place to baptize children! In the end, the hostility that his arrogance breeds results in the death of his youngest daughter and turns the entire community against him.

Kingsolver has the novelist's gift for emphasizing the obvious and helping us to see it again clearly. It is impossible for Nathan Price to plant the seeds of community in this African village because his own marriage is a rejection of the kind of relationships that make community possible. We rightly assume that Christian community shapes us as married couples and unmarried singles, but the opposite is important as well. Christian marriage, where love and power are shared, forms us into individuals who can appreciate the gifts of both genders. Single Christians can be shaped by their individual relationships with members of the other sex in a way that makes them loving members in the larger body. God empowers us to build communities of men and women in various ways; certainly not least of these is the way in which, in our marriages and other primary relationships, we understand the full equality of all people in Jesus Christ.

Community
and Christian Freedom

1 Corinthians 8–10

Paul's words in chapters 8–10 of this letter to the Corinthians have much
in common with his words in chapters 5 and 6. Both passages deal with
the relationship between church and world and consider how ethical
issues affect the community. However, in these two sections Paul shows
that Christian freedom operates differently in different situations. In
chapters 5 and 6, Paul rejects the Corinthians' notion that they are free
to ignore an incestuous relationship and to frequent brothels. In chapters 8–10, on the other hand, Paul agrees with the Corinthians who say
that they are free to eat meat that has been sacrificed to idols. He writes
this long and complicated section to help the Corinthians to grasp what
it means to be free in Jesus Christ and to understand the nature of Christian freedom, especially in terms of how that freedom might adversely
affect community.

Once again, Paul is discussing an issue that is dividing the Corinthian
community. In this case, the barrier to community is certain "knowing"
Christians' assumption that they can pursue their individual rights without regard to how their actions might affect others in the church. It is
hard to imagine a passage that is more attuned to the particular community issues we face as American Christians. In a society where personal freedom is valued to the extreme and the dangers of idolatry are
ignored, the Christian communities we find ourselves in are too often
split between those who fail to recognize the limits of freedom and those
whose fear of freedom produces a legalistic type of Christianity.

1 Corinthians 8

Food sacrificed to idols (1 Corinthians 8:1) was a lightning-rod issue for Gentile Christians in the early church. This food, especially meat, was sacrificed to pagan gods and then either eaten in the temple proper at cultic meals or social gatherings, or sold in temple meat markets for consumption at home.[1] Did participating in any of these activities compromise the Christian faith? New Testament witnesses other than Paul reject association with food that so clearly symbolizes the Gentiles' former religious lives. In Revelation 2:14 and 20 the practice is condemned and put on a level with fornication. In Acts 15:19–21 we read that James gives the minimum ethical requirements for Gentile Christians: they are free from most requirements of the Jewish law, but they must "abstain . . . from things polluted by idols" (15:20).

Paul's letters, however, indicate that this issue was far from cut-and-dried. We cannot tell whether Paul disobeyed the pronouncements of James and the Jerusalem council or simply did not know about them (see Paul's version of the council and its findings in Galatians 2:1–10), but we do know from Romans 14 and 1 Corinthians 8–10 that Paul believed that Gentile Christians had considerable freedom in these matters. In fact, by taking a liberal approach to the matter of such food ("the earth and its fullness are the Lord's," 10:26; cf. Romans 14:14, 20), and perhaps even eating this food himself in the homes of his friends at Corinth, Paul may well have precipitated the community issue he must now address.

The two groups involved in this discussion about meat sacrificed to idols are almost caricatures of modern liberal and conservative Christians. Members of the "liberal" group are able to rationalize that their freedom has no bounds. On the basis of their knowledge of the oneness of God (8:4–6), they believe that they have the right to eat sacrificial meat even in pagan temples (8:10) and without concern for how their actions might affect their fellow Christians (8:7–13) or endanger their own spiritual lives (10:14–22). Members of the "conservative" group, usually called "the weak" because of the way Paul describes them in verses 8:7–13, are much more wary of sacrificial meat. They try to avoid it completely, even, apparently, when it is served in private homes (see the discussion in 10:23–11:1). The weak rightly understand the dangerous link between sacrifical meat and their former pagan lives, preferring, at least here, ethical absolutes to freedom. Paul writes primarily to protect this group, those who believe that idols stand behind this temple meat and who are therefore prone to temptation when they see other Christians dining in pagan temples (8:9–13).

On the basis of the research of New Testament scholar Gerd Theissen, it is probably best to see these two groups as a reflection of class differences in the Corinthian church.[2] The more prominent and wealthy members would have more regularly eaten expensive idol meat in their homes and would have been more frequent guests at temple social functions. Not only would it have been difficult for them to give up what had become a regular part of their lives, but the commonplace nature of food sacrificed to idols may have more easily convinced them that it had no real religious significance. The poor, on the other hand, able to eat such meat only on rare occasions of cultic significance, would have understood it primarily in relationship to idols and their temples. Indications of class tensions appear several times in 1 Corinthians (see my earlier discussion regarding 1:16–31 and 6:1–11), and will receive attention again as a community issue in our discussion of 11:17–34.

Responding to another of the inquiries the Corinthians made in their recent letter (8:1; cf. 7:1), Paul quotes and agrees with the "freedom" party in a number of areas. It is true that all Christians should possess knowledge about the nature of food sacrificed to idols (8:1), specifically that "no idol in the world really exists" and that "there is no God but one" (8:4). And Paul must admit that "food will not bring us close to God" (8:8; the last clause in v. 8 may be a quote of the Corinthians just as these other assertions are). But the apostle realizes that in this case the knowledge that is determining the ethical stance of the freedom party is both limited and self-serving. Members of the party fail to grasp either the religious power of cultic meals (10:14–22) or how their selfish expression of liberty is affecting others in the community (8:9–12).

Paul devastates the position of the freedom party by asserting at the very beginning of his argument that "knowledge puffs up, but love builds up" (v. 1). This is one of the most powerful one-liners about Christian community found anywhere in his letters. The misguided knowledge of the freedom party is a sign of arrogance because it allows them to be entirely self-centered in their judgments and actions. Their assessment of the situation is the only thing that matters to them. This is not the first time Paul has accused certain of the Corinthians of being puffed up. In 5:2 he describes some Corinthians as arrogant because they claim the right to ignore the immorality in their midst, unconcerned with how it might affect the community. And in chapter 4 (vv. 6, 18–19) Paul chides the Corinthians for their arrogance because their desire for the wisdom that comes in rhetorically sophisticated sermons is splitting the church into camps.

Love, on the other hand, is *not* puffed up (13:4). It "builds up" (*oikodomeō*); that is, it seeks the good of the other and hence of the entire community (see Paul's use of the word in 10:23; 14:4, 12; 2 Corinthians

12:19; 13:10). The nature of this love is illustrated throughout this section of the letter. Love willingly sacrifices legitimate freedoms if they
endanger fellow Christians (8:9–13). Because of his love, Paul relin-
quishes individual rights (9:1–18; cf. 10:28–29) and seeks ways to serve
(9:19–27). Most important, love grows out of an imitation of Christ
(11:1). In a not-so-subtle jab at the freedom party, Paul insists that those
who claim to know actually remain ignorant (8:2). What is important
is not our knowledge, but the fact that God knows us in our love relationship (8:3). Love lies at the heart of our communion both with God
and with our fellow Christians.

Paul does not disagree with the theological content of the Corinthians'
knowledge, but he attempts to show them what their statement about
monotheism means when applied to this particular communal issue. Of
course these so-called gods do not really exist (v. 4), but Paul's aside in
verse 5 ("in fact there are many gods and many lords") raises an important point of consideration: for many people, idols do have a powerful
spiritual reality. The apostle's version of the Shema (v. 6)[3] critiques the
cold dogmatism of the freedom party.[4] Not only is there one God and
one Lord, Jesus Christ (note Paul's alteration of Deuteronomy 6:4), but
believers *belong* to this God. We exist for the Father (*eis auton*) and
through Jesus Christ (*di' autou*). Making an ethical decision is not simply a matter of extrapolating a theological principle, but also of ascer-
taining whether in one's actions one sins against Christ (8:12) or enrages
a jealous God (10:22).

The heart of Paul's argument, especially as it relates to Christian community, comes in 8:7–13. Even though, at least in theory, all members
of the Corinthian church understand that idols have no real existence
(8:1), many are unable to put this knowledge into practice. Old links
between idol food and idols are impossible to forget (v. 7). Their con-
science (*syneidēsis*), perhaps better understood here as moral self or
consciousness, is easily defiled. Watching the freedom party eat this sacrifical food in pagan temples (v. 10) does not enable them to grasp the
new freedom they have in Christ. Far from it. Instead, it actually tempts
them to return to idolatry. Like a recovering addict's craving for his drug,
the power of these Corinthians' former idolatrous lives makes dining in
pagan temples an impossible risk.

Paul makes it clear that the freedom party is endangering the community because it is acting on the basis of knowledge, not love. A correct knowledge of the oneness of God should liberate Christians from
any fear of food offered to idols. But this freedom must not become a
right with which they are obsessed and that they practice without consideration for its impact on fellow Christians. "Take care," Paul says to
those demanding freedom at all costs, "that this liberty of yours does

not somehow become a stumbling block to the weak" (v. 9). Love would not have allowed those in the freedom party to pursue a course so dangerous to their fellow Christians. This is not simply a case in which the assertion of rights leads to interpersonal conflict. Eating sacrificial meat in the temple districts has the potential of leading others away from Christ (they are "destroyed" [v. 11]). Such an act is a sin both against a member of one's Christian family (v. 12; literally, a brother) and against Christ, the one who died for them (vv. 11–12). Paul is using the strongest possible language to show that selfish freedom can put the Christian lives of those around us at risk. In Christian community freedom must be governed by love.

The last verse in chapter 8 is a transition to Paul's argument throughout chapter 9, in which he uses his own lifestyle as an example of the proper expression of Christian freedom. Paul states that he would give up meat altogether, not just food tainted by association with pagan temples, if his eating meat became a problem for those in his community. Paul's personal example of his relinquishment of rights is central to his argument about the nature of Christian freedom, but it is also important because it helps us to understand how chapter 8 relates to Paul's train of thought in this larger section of the letter (8:1–11:1). This question has been the subject of perennial scholarly debate. Chapter 9 logically follows chapter 8, but the transition to 10:1–22 is more difficult. Instead of speaking of an act that is governed by freedom and the limitations imposed by love, his apparent position in chapter 8, Paul now treats the eating of food sacrificed to idols as something that is absolutely forbidden (see 10:14–22). And the transition to 10:23–11:1 is no less abrupt. Paul suddenly begins talking about freedom again, even encouraging the Corinthians to eat this idol meat when it is served at private meals (10:27). Exactly how does chapter 8 fit into the larger discussion?

Older commentaries tended to associate chapter 8 with 10:23–11:1, assuming that in both Paul is concerned with an act that is governed by freedom, purchasing idol meat in temple "grocery stores" and eating it at home. Current scholarship, rightly noting that the eating described in chapter 8 occurs "in the temple of an idol" (v. 10), often equates it with the participation in the cultic meals described in 10:1–22. But this creates another problem. How can Paul speak of eating in the temple of an idol as an issue of freedom in chapter 8, only to expressly forbid it in 10:1–22? Many scholars now think that it is Paul's strategy to first discuss the issue in terms of its communal impact (chapter 8), and only then to address its ethical legitimacy (10:1–22).[5] From the point of view of Christian community, this is a very attractive option indeed: Paul first tries to convince the Corinthians that they must avoid idol food because it is dangerous to their fellow Christians, and only thereafter does he declare his "no."

While this is a possible solution, it is also problematic because it downplays Paul's personal examples. Beginning already in 8:13, Paul illustrates what he has said about eating food sacrificed to idols by pointing out the legitimate freedoms he has been willing to sacrifice as an apostle. His analogies could only be heard by the Corinthians as an indication that their use of this sacrifical food is governed by Christian liberty—liberty that, of course, must be guided by love. And Paul uses the same word to describe his rights (*exousia*; see 9:4–6, 12, 18) that he employs for those of the Corinthians in chapter 8 (v. 9). In chapter 9 this word becomes a synonym for the more common term for freedom (*eleutheros*, 9:1, 19). Paul is not arguing in chapter 8 "as if" the Corinthians were free in this matter. Christians have real freedoms in Jesus Christ, but freedoms that are willingly sacrificed in communal love.

As noncontemporaries reading the Corinthians' mail, it is important that we remind ourselves that our knowledge of the historical situation Paul is addressing is extremely limited. While there is some logic in linking chapter 8 with 10:1–22, it is possible that the two passages address separate problems in the church (between which, of course, the Corinthians would have been able to distinguish). There is no reason that Paul could not have been addressing at least three different ways of eating meat offered to idols: buying meat in the temple grocery store and eating it at home (10:27: don't worry about it); eating meat in the temple at cultic feasts (10:14–22: strictly avoid it); and eating meat in the temple in some less dangerous situation, perhaps at a social function (8:10: avoid it if it causes a fellow Christian to stumble).

1 Corinthians 9

As the Corinthians' spiritual father (4:14–21), Paul can think of no more graphic example than his own sacrifice among them, especially that of foregoing the right to be paid for ministerial duties (9:1–14). If Paul sounds defensive here (see vv. 2–3), it is probably because some at Corinth were suspicious of an apostle so at odds with established practice. Apparently most other apostles were so well compensated they could even bring their wives along (v. 5). Paul agrees that compensation for ministry is a right. Because he is writing to a church that would have preferred to pay its pastor, his long argument in support of this right seems like overkill. In support of the practice, Paul musters common sense (v. 7), the law of Moses (vv. 8–12), the practice of Jewish priests (v. 13), and even the words of Jesus (v. 14; see Luke 10:7). But it is precisely Paul's point that the inviolability of this right makes his willingness to give it up all the more significant (vv. 12, 15). Although we do not know the specific reasons why he avoided pay,[6] Paul is making it clear to the Corinthians that he did not want to "put any obstacle in the way of the gospel of Christ" (v. 12).

In what sense then is Paul free? After hearing this statement about rights relinquished, some in the freedom party must have thought to respond to the apostle's rhetorical "Am I not free?" (v. 1) by saying "No, you are not." But Paul's point in 9:15–23 is that freedom needs to be redefined; it is not the grasping of individual rights (v. 15), or self-adulation (boasting, [v. 16]), or the setting up of exclusivist social boundaries (vv. 19–22). Rather, Christian freedom is found in obedience to Christ, in the emptying of self and in service to others.

For Paul, freedom has ironically come in obligation, in an irresistible call to serve Christ. The language of 9:15–23 is that of stewardship, even slavery. Proclaiming the gospel is a necessity (*anangkē*, v. 16; translated "obligation" in the NRSV). Paul has been "entrusted with a commission" (*oikonomia*, v. 17). He has enslaved himself to all for the sake of the gospel (v. 19), and he is now controlled by the law of Christ (v. 21). This is probably Paul's way of emphasizing that Christian freedom is not a license to sin, but a mandate to serve (see Galatians 6:2).

Even though Paul briefly mentions his freedom relative to other people (v. 19) and the Torah (v. 20; cf. Galatians 3–5, where law is the key issue), his primary concern as he addresses this headstrong freedom party at Corinth is freedom from self. The Paul who was called by the risen Christ has been freed from an agenda of self-promotion. He no longer has to carefully guard his own rights or protect his social status. Paradoxically, Paul is free to give up his own freedoms. Christian freedom, in the fuller sense of the word, means the freedom to follow Christ, the freedom to love and serve those around us in a way that would have been impossible in our previously self-centered world. The Corinthians need to be reminded that only when they live as people who "are not your own" and who "were bought with a price" (6:19–20) can they experience the true freedom that comes in Christian service.

Paul is less explicit here than he is in certain other places about how Christ is the source and model for this radical freedom (see, for example, Philippians 2:1–11; Galatians 3–5), but he does give obvious indications that his freedom to serve is a response to Christ. Apart from the language of call already mentioned, Paul makes it clear in the final line of this section (11:1) that the life of Christian freedom grows out of an imitation of Christ. Here Paul is so bold as to encourage the Corinthians to imitate him, confident that his life reflects the kind of freedom exemplified in Christ. The best indication that the freedom Paul is speaking of has a rich christological foundation lies precisely in the way he describes his own life of service, especially in 9:19–23. Like Christ, who entered our world and emptied and humbled himself (Philippian 2:7–8), Paul has relinquished rigid self-definitions so that he might "become all things to all people" (9:22). This former Pharisee and persecutor of the church has been so liberated that he can ignore issues of personal status and race as he tries to bring diverse peoples to Christ. He can live among and minister to both Jews (v. 20) and Gentiles (v. 21). He has even become one of the "weak" (v. 22); this is probably another reference to the lower-class Christians at Corinth who are wary of idol meat (8:7–12). Paul's ministry is ample evidence that Christ can free a person to love.

In the final paragraph of chapter 9 Paul uses the familiar athletic metaphor to drive the point home (vv. 24–27). The Corinthians who have exercised their freedom recklessly need the self-control of a winning athlete (v. 25), the kind of direction and discipline that Paul, now pictured as a runner or boxer, illustrates in his ministry (v. 26). And so Paul's focus is once again on members of the freedom party and how they must conduct themselves. His autobiographical response to them in chapter 9 is a marvelous statement about the nature of Christian freedom. This freedom is not the mindless pursuit of individual rights, which is toxic to community. Rather, as Paul's ministry shows, it is the liberty that comes to those who have been transformed by Christ, those who are less concerned with their own rights and status than with how their actions build up the community. Paul's response to the Galatians, applied in that epistle to quite a different kind of freedom issue, would have been appropriate here as well: "Do not use your freedom as an opportunity for self-indulgence, but through love become slaves to one another" (5:13).

1 Corinthians 10

Although the transitions to the two topics discussed in chapter 10 are far from smooth (10:1 and 10:23; some scholars have even suggested that these sections are later interpolations), Paul's logic surely would have been clear to his Corinthian readers. After he concludes his long personal example by focusing again on the responsibility of the freedom party (9:24–27), Paul continues to speak to these proponents of freedom (10:1–22). Now, however, his concern is not how their eating of idol meat might affect the "weak," but how they themselves are in danger of sliding into idol worship. Paul's logic soon becomes clear: he uses the case of Israel as an example of how spiritual overconfidence might lead to idolatry. Similar to the Christian sacraments of baptism and the Lord's Supper, signs of God's grace were received by the Israelites in their deliverance from Egypt and march to the Promised Land (vv. 1–4).[7] But these actions of God on their behalf did not prevent them from slipping into idolatry (vv. 7–8; see Exodus 32; Numbers 25), just as Christ's blessings upon the Corinthians do not make them impervious to temptation. Paul's warning to the spiritually confident freedom party is clear: "So if you think you are standing, watch out that you do not fall" (v. 12).

Applied to the specific issue Paul is addressing, this means that the Corinthians must beware that they do not actually worship idols by participating in pagan cultic meals (vv. 14–22). Although the kind of eating discussed in 8:7–13 is an issue of freedom, participation in cultic meals is strictly forbidden. But if idols have no real existence, as both the freedom party and Paul agree (see 8:4), how can the so-called worship of idols be dangerous? Here Paul's argument must have seemed to the Corinthians like an interpretive sleight of hand, but it is entirely consistent with his apocalyptic worldview. Demons lie behind idols (vv. 19–20; cf. Deuteronomy 32:17). There is indeed but one God (8:4), yet Paul, like Jesus (see Mark 3:20–27 and parallels), is acutely aware of Satan's power in these end times. At one point in 2 Corinthians, Paul even calls God's opponent in this cosmic battle "the god of this world" (4:4). To worship idols is to play with fire.

In his attempt to get the Corinthians to grasp the seriousness of this matter, Paul uses an image that should be convincing (as "sensible people" they can judge what he says for themselves [v. 15]): the fellowship with the deity that occurs in the sacred meal. Just as the Lord's Supper brings a fellowship or communion (*koinōnia*; "sharing" in the NRSV) in the blood and body of Christ (v. 16) and Israel's sacrificial meals makes the participants "partners in the altar" (*koinōnos*; v. 18), so those who partake of pagan cultic meals become "partners with demons" (*koinōnos*; v. 20). Although Paul does not theologize about the nature of this fellowship (for the Lord's Supper, see 11:23–26), it is clear that it represents an exclusive relationship with the divine host. Participation in a cultic meal is a declaration of commitments made and benefits received. It is impossible, Paul says, to have fellowship with demons and still expect to have fellowship with Christ (v. 21). The God who is our beginning and end (8:6) jealously guards our relationship with him (v. 22). Christian freedom clearly has its limits.

If Paul's concern in chapter 8 was the communal basis for the proper exercise of Christian freedom, in 10:1–22 it is the spiritual danger encountered by those who assume there are no ethical absolutes in the Christian life. But even here Paul cannot resist at least alluding to the community implications of this abuse of freedom. Those who link them-selves to the demonic in pagan cultic meals not only risk their relation-ship with the Christ who gave his blood and body for us (v. 16) but also put the unity of the body of Christ as *community* in jeopardy (v. 17). It is no accident that Paul refers to the elements of the Lord's Supper in reverse order (v. 16; cf. 11:23–25). By mentioning the body of Christ sec-ond, he can more easily expand upon it as an image for the unity of the community. The many who eat the one bread and share in the body of Christ become one body (v. 17), held together by their relationship with a loving Christ and hence by their love for one another. It is most cer-tainly Paul's reference to *koinōnia* in verse 16 that triggers this short excursus on community. For him, Christian fellowship is always both what we share in Jesus Christ (see 1:9 and this volume's introduction) and how we share in one another's lives as a result of these blessings, a communion with Christ and inevitably with other believers.

Paul does not stop to tell his readers exactly how this reckless use of freedom endangers the one body, but the implications are clear. By becoming partners with demons they exclude themselves from the fel-lowship in Christ, diminishing the body and depriving the community of their gifts. Perhaps it is this brief reference to the incomplete body that confirms in Paul's mind the value of the image, and he quickly employs it again. In 11:17–34, also in the context of a discussion of the Lord's Supper, Paul talks about divisions in the body of Christ that are based on class differences. And in 12:12–31 Paul talks about the com-munity as body in terms of both its unity and diversity. In the present argument, Paul's impromptu discussion of the one body in 10:17 shows just how close to the surface his thoughts about community lie. Mem-bers of the freedom party need to know that their flirtation with the lim-its of freedom is a threat not only to their personal salvation but also to the integrity of the community.

In his final words (10:23–11:1) in this section about freedom, Paul summarizes his thoughts on the matter (10:23–24 and 10:31–11:1) and comments briefly on a related but distinct issue, the practice of buying meat sacrificed to idols at the market and eating it at home (vv. 25–30). The transition to this passage is rough indeed. Paul has just asserted that certain acts are off-limits for Christians. How can he now quote and apparently agree with the freedom party's motto, "All things are lawful" (v. 23; cf. 6:12)? The obvious answer is that Paul has shifted gears and is now summarizing his thoughts about Christian conduct in situ-ations in which freedom does apply.

The Corinthians need to hear again in a decisive way what Paul has already said several times: Christian freedom must be tempered by love for others. Their mantra about freedom, though legitimate, is not complete. "All things are lawful," but not all things are beneficial, nor do all things build up the community (see 8:1). Personal freedom is not an end in itself. Verse 24 of chapter 10 is one of the clearest and most radical statements about community relations found anywhere in Paul's writings: "Do not seek your own advantage, but that of the other." Love expressed in self-sacrifice is the glue that holds community together. Christians imitate the love they see in Jesus Christ (11:1), the kind of incarnational and self-giving love that becomes, as Paul has shown in chapter 9, the most essential freedom of all.

It is important to keep in mind that Paul's corrective for the Corinthians does not mean he views their newfound Christian liberty as an insignificant thing. He does not deny that they have been freed in a powerful way. No longer do they have to cower before idols or feel the apprehension that comes from seeing a god behind every tree or rock. In fact, Paul's comment about sacrificial food eaten at home (10:25–30) is a clear reminder, now at the conclusion of his argument, of the superstitions they have left behind. And the lack of parallels in our modern world must not blind us to the radicalness of Paul's words: most Christians, whether of Jewish or Gentile origin, and all Jews would have strictly avoided such meat. Paul's interpretation of Psalm 24:1 ("the earth and its fullness are the Lord's," 10:26) is liberal by first-century standards (cf. Romans 14:14), and it is precisely how the freedom party would have employed the verse.

While most of 8:1–11:1 is directed toward those who abuse Christian freedom, it is hard to avoid the feeling that Paul wrote 10:25–30 with side-glances toward the "weak." It is quite possible that the Corinthian community has also been threatened by those who manipulate by claiming weakness. Imagine the tension in a church where some people, wary of Christian freedom, denounce even those who eat sacrificial meat in their homes, while others feel no compunction about participating in pagan cultic meals. Paul seems to be caught in the cross fire. His apparently defensive statements in 10:29–30 probably indicate that he has been judged by the weak for his liberal position; at the same time, his relinquishing of rights (9:4–23) and his association with the weak (9:22) may indicate that he has been critiqued by the freedom party as well (see 9:1–3).

Paul wants the Corinthians, and especially the weak, to know that they need not fear this sacrificial food. "Eat whatever is set before you" (10:27), he tells them. Yet even here, where there is no question about the legitimacy of the act, the apostle makes it clear that freedom must not eclipse one's concern for others in the community. If someone informs them that the food they are about to eat "has been offered in sacrifice" (v. 28), they are to avoid it. We wish that Paul had explained himself more fully here. Who is the informant: a pagan servant or one of the weak in the Corinthian church? More important, what is the issue? Would eating this meat give a deceptive picture of the church to a pagan? Would it upset a weaker member and therefore lead to conflict (unlike in 8:11–12, there is no mention of destroying someone spiritually)? If the later is true, can freedom survive in an environment where it is so easily manipulated by others?

Paul does not answer these questions for us, but it is clear in 10:28 that his primary concern (both here and throughout this larger section) is not the preservation of freedom, as important as that is in the Christian life, but the loving practice of freedom in the context of community. Especially on the basis of his personal examples in chapter 9, Paul is seeking to redefine freedom for the Corinthians. Christian freedom is freedom from self, freedom from the compulsion to always assert one's rights. True freedom comes in imitating the Christ who died for us on a cross (11:1), in living a life of love and service for others.

Paul's closing words of command (10:31–11:1) echo his larger argument and his own example: out of concern for the salvation of others, the members of the Corinthian congregation should avoid offending the diverse groups in the church, and they should worry less about their own rights (10:32–33). In other words, they should build up the community through love (8:1; 10:23). All of their conduct must be motivated by the desire to glorify God (10:31), a wonderful way of affirming that the freedom that expresses itself in love for the community is indeed an act of worship (cf. Romans 12:1).

Paul's Words for the Contemporary Community

1 Corinthians 8–10 is hardly a comprehensive statement about Christian freedom, even though our confusion about freedom, especially as American Christians, might make us wish it were. As is usually the case, Paul's words are limited because they are directed toward the specific issue he is addressing, in this case the communal impact of eating meat offered to idols. Absent is a discussion of the pivotal issue in his letter to the Galatians: freedom from the law, a kind of freedom that Christians can never relinquish because it is so central to the faith (Paul alludes to it in 1 Corinthians 9:21). Nor is Paul much help in defining essential human rights, although his discussion of pastoral support in chapter 9 indicates he is aware of this issue. Still, I am always amazed at how Paul's words, contextually bound as they are, continue to speak to the American church. In communities that are often divided between those who are fearful of freedom and those who abuse it, Paul's words

about freedom, and especially about its limitations, are important indeed.

Freedom and Its Limits

Considering the problem at Corinth, the abuse of freedom, Paul's attitude toward the eating of meat sacrificed to idols is rather surprising. He continues to affirm that the consumption of this meat is governed by Christian freedom, even though such a stance might play into the hands of the freedom party, and even though it most certainly puts him in conflict with a majority of Christians in the early church, those who accepted the ruling of the Jerusalem council (see Acts 15:19–21). This passage powerfully illustrates how important Christian freedom is for Paul. Our salvation in Jesus Christ has freed us from the restraints of the law—this is the message of Galatians and Romans—and has freed us to experience God's world with boldness and joy: "the earth and its fullness are the Lord's" (10:26, a paraphrase of Psalms 24:1 and 50:12).

Over the years several of my seminary students from Taiwan, China, and Korea have told of firsthand experiences with meat dedicated to the gods (especially by adherents to Taoism and popular religions) and taken home for consumption (as in 10:25–27). In many instances, they and their Christian families chose to avoid this meat completely because of its association with idols. When reminded of Paul's words in 10:25–26 (and, of course, Romans 14), they have often replied that Paul is a little too liberal, a little too open to this world. I do not pretend to understand all the contextual issues that have influenced these Asian Christians' decision to avoid such meat, but their assessment of Paul is telling and accurate. Paul *is* boldly liberal here. Even as he tries to limit the freedom of those who use it in a destructive way, his affirmation of the radical freedom of the Christian life is unmistakeable.

Paul's recognition of the importance of Christian freedom and his attempt to convince the weak to be more relaxed about sacrificial meat raise an issue that lies just beneath the surface in this passage. At what point do the protests of the weak become a barrier to community? At what point do the fears of the cautious become manipulative, dividing the community and preventing it from experiencing the joys and risks of Christian freedom? It is not difficult to make a long list of issues in the modern church concerning which people who are wary of freedom might sabotage the best interests of the community: new expressions of worship, particularly that bugaboo contemporary music; outreach in the church's neighborhood or civic community (for example, establishing a day care center), especially if it means involvement with secular organizations; new forms of Christian education that take the world seriously (for example, an adult class that studies modern cinema or novels); youth group sleepovers, and the form of entertainment at such events; contemporary architecture, and so on.

The point is not that a community should always pursue what freedom allows, but that the course it takes must reflect the concerns of all, not just the concerns of those whose fear of the unknown makes them the most vocal. Invariably this group has tremendous power in the church, in large part because it has inertia on its side. It too needs to hear that its arguments are fallible and, most important, that its position might have to be sacrificed out of love for the body.

Paul's affirmation of freedom and his belief that Christians can boldly enter and experience God's world make his pronouncements about sacrificing freedom all the more significant. And according to Paul, it is community and one's concern for the spiritual welfare of the Christian family that warrants this sacrifice. Where in the modern Christian life do we find parallels to what Paul is discussing in 1 Corinthians 8? Where might we have to curtail our expression of freedom because it might lead to idolatry in our fellow Christians?

The answers I typically hear are correct, but perhaps a bit too obvious to be very helpful. Christians who feel they are free to consume alcohol, participate in gambling, and experience the full gamut of society's cinematic, musical, and visual arts are usually quite aware of the impact these activities might have on community members. Following the lead of a fellow Christian in any of the above could prove to be disastrous for some. But I wonder if these often-mentioned dangerous freedoms are really the ones that most threaten us as American Christians; after all, even outside the church we are frequently reminded of the risks they pose.

More subtly dangerous is the way our participation in the world may influence fellow Christians to accept uncritically the American cultural ethos, the unwritten principles that shape our life in this country. In his book *How Does America Hear the Gospel?* William Dyrness discusses several of the values that lie at the heart of American culture, emphasizing especially pragmatic materialism, optimism, and individualism. Pragmatic materialism, to focus on just the first of these, grows out of a frontier mentality and finds support in the writings of such thinkers as John Locke, Ralph Waldo Emerson, and William James. Here truth is determined by what works. People realize their dignity in hard labor, especially work on the land, which is seemingly in endless supply, and the pursuit of landownership forces people to adapt to change and to solve problems efficiently. The American frontier that gives rise to this pragmatism is one of movement and spatial isolation; it defines people in terms of productivity and the rewards of work. Dyrness suggests that this pragmatic materialism affects modern American culture in at least three important ways. We are a culture that is "on the move": we assume that movement or change will invariably lead to a better job, a better marriage, or greater freedom. It becomes hard to distinguish progress from movement. Also, we are a culture that is in a hurry. We rush from task to task or from recreation to recreation, thinking that efficiency and volume can take the place of relationships and relaxation. Finally, we as a culture use things up.[8] Not only are we highly materialistic, but we also view possessions as things that can be devoured because they are easily replaced. We measure success in terms of accumulation and consumption.

Assuming, at least for the moment, that we can participate in this culture unscathed, where might our freedom lead to spiritual problems for some in our Christian family? Of course, our answer must be determined by context, by our knowledge of where our fellow Christians are vulnerable (as was so in the Corinthian church). Most important, a response that is based on 1 Corinthians 8 will not underestimate the ways in which a culture can become idolatrous. As we participate in our pragmatically materialistic culture, could it be that a promotion and move might have to be rejected because of what they might model for the community (including the biological family)? At what point do our incredibly busy lives demonstrate priorities that become a danger to the vulnerable in our communities? Is it possible that our use of material things might beckon fellow Christians to be less fearful of the idolatry of materialism or more apt to be destructive of God's creation? And we must not forget that our lives serve as examples in the cumulative sense, not just in specific, dramatic instances. Think of how a lifetime of uncritical participation in the materialism of American culture could numb others to its dangers, especially our children.

Being involved in the world is important, but our expression of Christian freedom must be guided by an awareness of its dangers. Lesslie Newbigin is right to warn us that we live in a society that is not simply secular, but pagan, and this pagan society is tough and resistant to the gospel because it was "born out of the rejection of Christianity."[9] Our freedom to participate in American society must be tempered by a healthy suspicion of what that society claims to be good, a suspicion that grows out of our love for community members who may be watching and following us.

With typical rhetorical flair, Martin Luther expresses the irony of Christian freedom: "A Christian is a perfectly free lord of all, subject to none. A Christian is a perfectly dutiful servant of all, subject to all."[10] For those who find their lordship in Jesus Christ, all other authorities are relativized. We are new creations (2 Corinthians 5:17), free to boldly enter a world that no longer constrains us by its definitions. Yet Paul reminds us that we are also servants of others in our community, ready to set aside that which we may be free to do or say when it threatens those we love. Of course, it is the second part of this paradoxical couplet that is the most radical. Paul's command, "Do not seek your own advantage, but that of the other" (10:24), is challenged in our world wherever we turn. From the competition of business and sports, to the eroticism of entertainment and the arts, to the self-serving love promoted by talk shows and relational gurus, society incessantly encourages us to do whatever it takes to make ourselves happy. As Christians seeking community we do well to remind ourselves just how unique our understanding of freedom is, and therefore how important a well-informed and critical view of American culture is.

Freedom Transformed

It should come as no surprise to us that the freedom we see practiced in the church often reflects that of American culture at large. Of course, our political system is based upon a particular understanding of freedom, especially the guarantee of individual rights. And other factors in the development of the American ethos ensure that freedom and individualism go hand in hand. Ours is an immigrant society, and freedom has meant the right to better oneself materially and socially. Our brand of pragmatic materialism suggests that we are free to pursue a material dream that is achieved through hard work and assertive self-promotion. Our unique experience of the "endless frontier" and the pursuit of the perfect homestead has given rise to a culture in which freedom means spatial independence. Good neighbors are defined in terms of good fences. The list could go on. We have uncritically wed ourselves to these and many other cultural influences, thus producing two views of freedom that seriously challenge Christian community: freedom as the pursuit of self-interest, and freedom as autonomy.

The chances are good that anyone who has served on a church committee or governing board will be able to attest to the destructive power of the pursuit of self-interest, the selfish attitude toward personal rights and power that declares "my way or no way." We feel free to defend our pet issues more assertively than we ought to; we intimidate those who disagree with us; and most divisive of all, we refuse to cooperate with the community when the vote goes against us. It only takes a few members who define freedom primarily as the pursuit of self-interest to create an atmosphere in which any group discussion or vote has the potential of splitting the communty. The kind of freedom that deafens us to those around us is especially a problem at the denominational level in most churches, where too often special interest groups vie for power as they try to influence policy. A healthy community gives me the freedom to lift my voice and the issue I represent, but if mine is the only voice the community can hear, then there is a problem. Freedom as the pursuit of self-interest, to put it in graphically American terms, means becoming a spiritual and ecclesiastical entrepeneur.

If freedom as the pursuit of self-interest manipulates community, freedom as autonomy ignores it. Freedom becomes independence; it seeks a certain required space that separates us from the other and relieves us from both responsibility and positive influence. In the church this expresses itself in the huge numbers who claim to be Christian but never join a worshiping community. They preserve their autonomy by watching televangelists and praying alone. But even sadder are those who seek isolation within the church: those who come to worship alone, who sit by themselves and leave quickly after the service, never participating in community functions where they would come face-to-face with fellow Christians. Spirituality, even when it is expressed in public worship, is divorced from community. Christian freedom as autonomy gives voice to the spiritual equivalent of the isolationist's ballad: "Give me land, lots of land, under open skies above; don't fence me in."

Paul's autobiographical comments in 1 Corinthians 9 directly challenge these expressions of freedom. This is one of those many places in Scripture where the message is so inconsistent with the cultural status quo that we need to beware lest our defense mechanisms lull us into a superficial reading. If Paul is free (and his rhetorical question in 9:1 indicates that he thinks he is), then this is a strange kind of freedom indeed. He is most free as he fulfills his call to serve Jesus Christ. Paul describes this call not with words we usually associate with liberation, but in terms that denote bondage and responsibility: endurance (v. 12), obligation (v. 16), commission (v. 17), slavery (v. 19), and law (v. 21). This freedom that comes in obedience to Christ liberates Paul from narrow self-interest. He is even free to give up something as important and self-defining as ministerial pay. Paul's freedom is not liberation from others; rather, it finds its fullest expression when he serves others for the gospel, even seeking out community with those who are very unlike himself (vv. 19–23).

It is sometimes said that freedom in our culture is primarily a freedom *from*, while Christian freedom is especially a freedom *for*. In contrast to those who seek freedom from want, from oppression, or even from responsibility, Christians seek to be free for service to Jesus Christ and all that that entails. But surely this is an incomplete definition. Christian freedom is a freedom both *from* and *for;* it is simply that what we leave behind and what we hope to experience make our liberation radically different from that of society. Paul models freedom from preoccupation with self, freedom from an addiction to individual rights. We are, as Paul's example shows us, free from society's effort to define us, and especially from the indifference and isolation that keep us from community. And as Christians we are free for obedience to Christ. We are free for service to the Christian community, even when this means, as in Paul's case, an incarnation among people who are unlike us. As Christians we have been freed for the fullest expression of who we are in our relationship with Christ and our fellow Christians.

It is important to keep in mind that Paul's autobiographical comments in chapter 9 are the words of someone who has been transformed. Paul has been changed, confronted by the risen Christ in the Damascus road experience (Galatians 1:15–17; 1 Corinthians 15:8; cf. Acts 9:1–22; 22:4–16; 26:9–18) and probably in other visions as well (see his description of one in 2 Corinthians 12:1–4). His old identity as a Pharisee has been so altered by his relationship with Christ that he actually thinks of himself as needing to *become* a Jew or *become* a person "under the law" (9:20) in his incarnational ministry. It is this spiritual transformation that is the basis of Paul's radical understanding of interpersonal freedom in the Christian community. For Paul, communal freedom and salvific freedom are not separable. Because we have been freed from the law as it is manipulated by sin (Galatians 3:19–22; Romans 7:12–13) and have thus been declared children of God (Galatians 4:1–7), we are now free, "through love," to "become slaves to one another" (Galatians 5:13).

Readers who have any doubts about the ultimate source for the freedom we practice in community are addressed in Paul's final words in this section: Christ is our model (11:1). But interestingly Paul affirms an indirect imitation of Christ. "Be imitators of me," Paul says, "as I am of Christ." Paul understands how important a fellow Christian's modeling of interpersonal freedom is for these immature Corinthians. A freedom so inconsistent with the status quo needs to be modeled in the community. It is important that we as modern Christians be able to point to heroes in the faith, people like Nelson Mandela, who after being imprisoned and abused for twenty-eight years was free to leave the hatred behind and free to serve those who had been his captors. Even more, we need to remind ourselves where this freedom is modeled in our midst. It is often most evident in Christian families who understand the give and take of long-term relationships motivated by love.

But what is so striking about Paul's words in 11:1, especially to those of us who are pastors, is the way he exhorts the Corinthians to imitate *him* and *his* expression of freedom. This command is neither foolhardy nor arrogant, although we often interpret it as such. It grows out of the genuine concern for the Corinthians that Paul has as the one who founded the church and is therefore responsible for it (see 4:14–21). Above all, it reflects the boldness of a person who is confident of his call and confident of the transformation that has occurred within him. Perhaps we should not be asking why Paul would say such a thing, but rather inquiring why we as Christian leaders so seldom do so. Are we afraid of the responsibility? Or are we fearful that those who observe us will see in us the same desire for self-interest and autonomy that is present in society's expression of freedom? Paul's words challenge us because we know that this strange freedom he espouses, this freedom for obedience, can only be realized by those who are willing to let Christ transform their lives.

"Something Immensely Missing"

The apostle makes it clear that the way we practice freedom not only affects others but also affects *us*, and in both cases there is a serious impact upon community. When faced with options that John Calvin calls "indifferent"[11] (*adiaphoroi*) or not inconsistent with the faith, our choice is guided by each option's potential for harming fellow Christians (1 Corinthians 8). But not all our options are innocuous. As Paul shows in his discussion about participation in pagan meals (10:1–22), we can make choices that separate us from the body of Christ.

Where in the American church does freedom lead its practitioners into an idolatry that is dangerous to community? In a collection of short stories entitled *The Afterlife and Other Stories*, John Updike, known for his graphic depiction of fallen humans wrestling with their spiritual alienation, creates portraits of elderly people who are facing death and the isolation and meaninglessness of their lives. Fogel, the main character in the story "Short Easter," is an especially good example of a person who expresses freedom as autonomy. Even though Fogel has a family and is financially secure, his life is empty. At sixty-two he is obsessed with the fleeting nature of life, angry because his body is growing old, angry at younger drivers who show him no respect, even angry that daylight savings time would steal an hour from Easter Sunday. Above all, Fogel is an incredibly self-centered person who has eliminated all meaningful relationships from his life. He sees his wife as a manipulative nag. He recalls an affair he had many years ago, not because he still loves the woman, but because he remembers the indignation that he, the jilted lover, felt when he was excluded from his mistress's annual Easter party. Although his wife has friends, he views the task of mingling with the other couples at a champagne brunch as an endurance test, one that necessitates a second Bloody Mary.[12]

Easter does remind Fogel of the church, but he does not act upon the vague, nostalgic attraction it casts. After a haunting, dream-filled nap on Easter afternoon, Fogel awakes in the shadows of an empty house with an "unnatural ache of resurrection—the weight, the atrocious weight, of coming to life again." This resurrection, however, makes a mockery of the person the day celebrates. Fogel wakes to continued fear and isolation, although he does not fully comprehend the extent of his living death. Lying in fetal position on the bed, Fogel peers into the growing darkness where everything appears to be as it was before, yet he is seized by an inexplicable terror when he realizes that "something was immensely missing."[13]

Certainly one of the greatest threats to Christian community in our society is the erroneous assumption that freedom means separation from others, or autonomy. Fogel's entire life has been a project of destroying relationships for his own benefit. He is, in the end, free, but free from community and therefore free from anything that gives life meaning. He has chosen an alternate community, one in which he is the only member.

Consistent with the implications of Updike's story, Paul reminds us in 1 Corinthians 10 that we may be faced with choices that lead to a communal either/or. Those who participate in pagan worship have made a choice about their membership in the "one body," the body of Christ (v. 17). Christian community is exclusive in the sense that it demands a decision about where our ultimate allegiance lies. We cannot dine at an idol's table and still eat with the Christian family; we cannot have fellowship with two communities at war with one another (vv. 20–21).

This means, of course, that even though we may be free to choose, not all of our choices lead to Christian freedom. Paul puts this in a slightly different way in Romans 6 when he says that we present ourselves as obedient slaves either to sin and death or to righteousness (vv. 15–19). Here Paul implies, as he does in 1 Corinthians 10, that in certain cases involving basic issues in the faith, we cannot avoid making a decision. At times we are like Neo in the science fiction movie *The Matrix*, who is forced by Morpheus to choose between his present existence, a drug-induced virtual slavery, and the risk-filled freedom of the real world.[14]

In light of Paul's emphasis on the importance and exclusiveness of Christian community, what do we say about ourselves when we pursue freedom as autonomy, when we intentionally isolate ourselves from fellow Christians? What do those half-empty sanctuaries on Sunday morning say about our choice? What—or better, who—is the focus of our idolatry when we go to such great lengths to protect ourselves from the messiness and joy of community? Discussing the world that the Old Testament prophets addressed, Abraham Heschel says that "the opposite of freedom is not determinism, but hardness of heart."[15] Could it be that the autonomy we assume to be a neutral separation from community is actually an intentional rejection of one of God's greatest gifts, a provoking of the God who jealously (10:22) seeks our fellowship in the body of Christ (10:16–17)?

Community
and Class Differences
1 Corinthians 11:17–34

It is unfortunately a common occurrence in the church: certain Scripture passages are widely used, but are often misinterpreted or applied inappropriately. First Corinthians 11:17–34 is one of these passages. The words of institution of the Lord's Supper, found in verses 23–26, often have a liturgical function, but when we use them we have no hint of the community issue Paul is addressing. Verses 27–32, about partaking of communion "in an unworthy manner," suffer a similar fate. Removed from the context of class tension in the Corinthian church (vv. 20–22), these verses are used to encourage personal introspection in preparation for the Lord's Supper, an application quite different from Paul's intent.

Recognizing the historical context of this passage does not necessarily make its application in the modern church easier. In fact, when we hear Paul's words as part of a first-century conversation, they can actually seem more remote, more alien to the modern ear. What are we supposed to do with Paul's apparent link between illness and the misuse of the sacrament (vv. 29–30)? If Paul's words relate to the celebration of the Lord's Supper as a full meal (vv. 21–22; 33–34), how do they apply to our abbreviated version of the sacrament? Most important, what can Paul's warning about the flagrant abuse of the poor by the rich within the Corinthian church possibly have to do with us, we who are products of American society, with its large middle class and its presumed equality?

In 1 Corinthians 11:17–34 Paul deals explicitly with a barrier to community that has surfaced several times before in this letter: tensions between social classes (1:26–31; chapter 6; chapters 8–10). The ease with

111

which we separate verses 23–26 from their context in 1 Corinthians indicates not only our willingness to disregard this particular community problem, but also, I think, our confusion about why Paul responds as he does. Why does Paul repeat the words of institution as his first line of defense against those who misuse their economic status? An honest interpretation of this passage may show that both the barrier Paul is addressing and the solution he offers have far more relevance for our Christian communities than we have been led to believe.

1 Corinthians 11:17–34

It is no accident that the conflict addressed in this passage is one of a series of community tensions that have their origin in the context of worship (11:2–16; 11:17–34; chapters 12–14; note the links to worship in chapters 1–4 and 8–10 as well). For Paul, community is not an abstract concept, but is something that happens when Christians gather; worship, the prime reason for gathering, is bound to be the locus of community problems. It is precisely when we rub shoulders that we rub people the wrong way. In the present passage Paul is so concerned with the quality of the worship gathering that he uses the word for "come together" five times (*synerchomai;* 11:18, 20, 33, 34; cf. 14:23, 26). It is interesting to note the way Paul combines a form of this verb with the term for "church" in verse 18 (*en ekklēsia;* "when you come together as a church"). In Paul's writings "church" is less an idea than an activity; it is what happens when Christians assemble under one roof to share gifts (12:27–31), hymns and proclamation (14:26–40), and love (13:4–13).[1] When Paul speaks of coming together as a church, he is being somewhat redundant, but it does illustrate his emphasis on issues that arise when Christians occupy the same space (cf. 11:20, which literally reads "when you come together in the same place").

The highly critical tone that pervades this passage is evident from the outset (11:17; cf. 11:2). Paul cannot commend the Corinthians for the way they celebrate the Lord's Supper because their actions do not create community, but destroy it ("it is not for the better but for the worse"; 11:17). Divisions (*schismata;* 11:18) have arisen. This is the exact term Paul uses to warn against factions in 1:10, but he is most certainly not addressing the same groups here. There the issue is splits generated by loyalty to rhetorically gifted leaders, by a desire for wisdom that occurs across class lines (see 1:26–31) and that may well pit one house church against another. Here the divisions pit poor against rich (11:22) and probably happen *within* house churches, the basic unit for the celebration of the Lord's Supper.

Paul's statement that he believes what he has heard "to some extent" (11:18) is an acknowledgment "that his informants are scarcely disinterested observers,"[2] not a way of downplaying the importance of this issue. His intentions are crystal clear: this perversion of worship must stop. Whatever they are doing, it cannot be called the Lord's Supper (v. 20)! The apostle's aside about the inevitability of church factions in the larger eschatological context (v. 19) might seem counterproductive to us (why seek unity at all?), but it surely would have come across as a warning to the offending parties at Corinth. What if they are not among the "genuine"? What if they are tested and found wanting (see vv. 31–32)?

In one or more of the house churches in Corinth, the wealthy, who have houses, fail to equitably share the meal that accompanies the Lord's Supper with the poor, those who have nothing (v. 22). For modern Christians, this issue needs to be unpacked in at least three ways. First of all, we need to realize that in the early church the Lord's Supper took place during or after a full meal. Celebrating the sacrament in this way is probably a reflection of the tradition, preserved in the Synoptic Gospels, that the original Last Supper was Jesus' reinterpretation of a Passover meal. Those of us who grow impatient with the minute portions of bread and wine we somehow dare to call "supper" can only imagine the spiritual and communal potential of such a feast.

Second, we need to understand how this meal is orchestrated in Corinth. It is logical to assume that house churches meet in the homes of their more wealthy members, because only those houses are large enough to accommodate the entire group of perhaps forty to sixty people. But we who are accustomed to the ample space of a church fellowship hall tend to forget the logistical and social issues involved in feeding this many people in a first-century Corinthian home. The typical dining room is only about eighteen feet square.[3] If this room is equipped with a triclinium (see John 2:8–9; the word translated "chief steward" is literally "head of the triclinium"), a three-sided table around which the diners recline, it would accommodate only about a dozen people. The rest of the church would be forced to eat in the adjoining courtyard, or atrium.

Who is invited to dine at the triclinium? Do these guests receive more or better food? Although the details elude us, Paul's hyperbolic language tells us that the poor went without while the rich overindulged (v. 21). It is not difficult to imagine a scenario in which the rich host, charged with providing both the place and the food for the gathering, gives his upper-class friends special treatment. High-status guests dine in comfort, close to the ice sculpture and champagne fountain, while the poor eat what little finds its way to the courtyard. Paul's words may even indicate that the rich members of the group have their own private little din-

ner party *before* the lower-class Corinthians arrive. He states that each
of the offenders "goes ahead" with the meal (v. 21; *prolambanō*), a translation that could be supported by Paul's later command that they "wait
for one another" (v. 33).

The third and perhaps most difficult thing for us to grasp about the
situation Paul is addressing is this: the social inequity found in the
Corinthian church is the norm, not the exception, in the first-century
Greco-Roman world. The high level of social stratification at this time
is perhaps best symbolized by a pyramid, with the few and powerful at
the top and the masses at the bottom.[4] Even the 75 percent of the population who are considered to be of low status fall into carefully delin-
eated ranks: artisans, merchants, urban and rural poor people, day
laborers, slaves, beggars, and so on. Upward mobility and social bonds
between people of different classes are relatively rare. A middle class as
we know it does not exist.

Paul's letter makes it clear that social stratification is a reality in the
Corinthian church as well. Often it expresses itself as a community problem. Our passage provides the most explicit example, but the issue concerning the use of courts (chapter 6) and the tension around eating meat
offered to idols (chapters 8–10) may also illustrate class conflict. In other
passages Paul simply acknowledges that different classes exist in the
church. He often names high-status people: Gaius, who hosts Paul and
has a house large enough for the entire Corinthian church (1:14; Romans
16:23); Erastus, a city treasurer (Romans 16:23), who may be the public official and patron named in an inscription found in Corinth; Crispus (1:14), a former synagogue ruler (Acts 18:8); Stephanas, the leader
of a household (1:16), who was free to travel in service of Paul (16:15);
and Aquila and Prisca, leaders of a house church (16:19).[5] Apart from
11:17–34, the clearest reference to lower classes in the Corinthian church
is found in 1:26–31. There Paul encourages certain Corinthians not to
pursue a kind of human wisdom that rejects both their own heritage
(1:26) and the "foolishness" of the cross. Paul's words in 7:21–24 may
indicate that the community included slaves.

Historical evidence suggests that the city of Corinth itself was no
stranger to class-consciousness. We know that when Corinth was
refounded by the Romans in 44 B.C.E. (it had been destroyed in 146
B.C.E.), it was settled primarily by "freedmen," former slaves who had
earned or had been given their freedom. Many of them became the new
rich, the entrepreneurs and wealthy business people of this prosperous
trade city. Our experience with American immigrant culture might lead
us to believe that Corinth would be a melting pot where equality was
valued, but the opposite appears to be true. Archeological discoveries
and the literature of the period indicate that Corinth was as hierarchi-

cal as any other Greco-Roman city of the period, and was unusual only
in that status was defined more by wealth than by family name (Erastus is a good example).⁶ Gerd Theissen even speculates that "in such an
aspiring city as this the social strata are *more* clearly differentiated from
one another than in places where from time immemorial there have
been well defined groups of wealthy families and groups of the poor."⁷

If social stratification is precisely what we should expect to find in
Corinth, then Paul's response to the way the church eats the sacramental meal represents the unexpected. His words are a clear challenge to
the cultural status quo. He tells the rich, those who are behaving as rich
people in that time normally do, that they show contempt for the church
of God and that they shame (v. 22; *kataischynō*; cf. its use in 11:4) those
who have nothing. The gospel of Jesus Christ redefines how rich and
poor will come together in community, just as it redefines relations
between women and men. The fact that Paul has heard about these tensions concerning the Lord's Supper indicates that there are protesters
in the Corinthian church, those who have understood the social rami-
fications of the good news. We must not forget that the Corinthian
church, with its inclusion of all classes, is already a unique community
by first-century standards. Nevertheless, the dispute addressed in
11:17–34 is yet another indication of the Corinthians' need to be resocialized, to be reshaped communally on the basis of the message of
Christ.

After Paul's high-voltage condemnation we might expect him to immediately tell the church how to remedy the situation (as he does in chapter 5). But his initial response is something quite different: he tells a
story! Paul carefully recounts Jesus' instructions about the Lord's Supper (vv. 23–25) and uses them as the basis for his imperative to the Corinthians (vv. 26–34). The apostle's precise use of the technical words
"received" and "handed on" (*paralambanō, paradidōmi;* note their parallel use in 15:3), coupled with his assertion that these words are "from
the Lord" (v. 23), serve notice that he is conveying the message of an
authoritative oral tradition. Why does Paul repeat and emphasize this
snippet from the story of the Last Supper the way he does, especially
since the Corinthians are already well aware of this exact form of the
words of institution?

It is impossible to hear verses 23–25 without thinking about the story
of the Last Supper and the way the larger gospel narrative leads
inevitably to Jesus' betrayal and death. These words focus the hearer on
the theological significance of Jesus' impending crucifixion. The serving of the bread and later the cup recalls the rites of Passover and thus
Israel's deliverance from slavery. Even more, Jesus reinterprets the
Passover rituals in terms of his own sacrifice. The broken bread repre-

sents his body that will be given *for* them (*hyper;* v. 24), a phrase Paul assumes is a reference to Christ's atonement for believers (see 15:3; Romans 5:6, 8; 2 Corinthians 5:21). The cup now represents Jesus' blood, shed on the cross (v. 25). Like blood shed in Old Testament animal sacrifice, this blood has atoning power (see Romans 3:25), and it also gives birth to the new covenant, a new relationship with God based upon Jesus' sacrifice (see Paul's discussion of the two covenants in 2 Corinthians 3:4–18).

Along with the story of the empty tomb and the resurrection appearances (as in 15:3–7), the words of institution form the core of the early oral tradition about Jesus. These words are recorded with amazing similarity in the Synoptic Gospels (Matthew 26:26–29; Mark 14:22–25; Luke 22:14–20; John mysteriously omits them), with Luke's version most closely resembling Paul's. In all of these passages Jesus commands that the rite be repeated, but only in Luke and Paul do we find the imperative, "Do this in remembrance of me" (11:24; Luke 22:19). Paul's version differs from Luke's especially in that he adds this "remembrance" clause a second time after the taking of the cup (v. 25). And in Paul alone we find an interpretive comment that gives his version of the words of institution an additional focus (v. 26): taking the bread and cup become a proclamation of the Lord's death in anticipation of his return.

It is very important to keep in mind that this is not simply random instruction about the Lord's Supper, but teaching that is intended to speak to a specific community problem. Paul emphasizes the words of institution the way he does because he wants the people at Corinth, especially the rich, to see again the Christ who stands behind the sacrament. Strictly speaking, Paul's words are more christological than sacramental. This is not an issue of liturgical niceties or a question of how Christ is present in the elements. The bread and cup point to a Christ who gave his life for us, a loving act of atonement. Removed from this context, the imperative to remember would perhaps be more sacramentally focused, a command to keep and repeat the Lord's Supper, consistent with Jesus' intent. But here the command to remember must refer to the necessity of comprehending the magnitude of God's gift in Jesus Christ. To remember means to recognize that one is part of a new covenant that has its origin in an act of radical love. It means that we boldly proclaim the foolishness of the cross (11:26; cf. 1:18–25). And most of all, to remember means that we live in community in a way that reflects the love we have received in Christ.

Few paragraphs better illustrate the importance of contextual interpretation than 11:27–32, where Paul gives the Corinthians concrete instructions concerning their dilemma. In light of the situation Paul is addressing, his warning to avoid coming to the table "in an unworthy manner" (v. 27) must point primarily to the rich and their abuse of the community. We can think of other transgressions that might trigger such a response in Paul; the behavior of the man living with his father's wife immediately comes to mind (chapter 5). But we must not suppose that Paul's words in 11:27 constitute a blanket prohibition against all who come unworthily. Paul is not trying to keep sinners from the Lord's Supper. If such were the case, none of the Corinthians (or us) could partake.

Yet this *is* another prime example of the seriousness with which Paul treats sins against the community. The Corinthians who promote these class distinctions during the Lord's Supper are said to be "answerable" for the Lord's body and blood (v. 27). This is not simply a reference to the desecration of the elements, although it is often interpreted as such. Paul's statement is actually far harsher; those who reject the poor in the church stand in opposition to the atoning love that Christ expressed on the cross (vv. 23–26). They become the enemies of Christ, and in that sense they are as liable for the death of Christ as those who originally arrested and betrayed him. Parallel to the function of the light in the Gospel of John (see especially 3:17–21), the cross in Paul becomes the ultimate touchstone of the Christian life. Christians who remember the cross manifest the sacrificial love of Christ in community, and those whose communal lives show that they have ignored the cross stand accused by it.

Considering the centrality of the theme of judgment in verses 27–32, it is no wonder that Paul exhorts the Corinthians to examine themselves before they partake of the sacrament (v. 28). But what sort of examination does Paul intend? In what is often considered the pivotal verse of this passage, Paul makes it clear that unless the Corinthians come to the Lord's Supper "discerning the body," their participation in the bread and cup incurs God's judgment (v. 29). The trouble is that the phrase "discerning the body" is ambiguous, especially to a modern church so quick to ignore the specific community problem Paul is addressing. It is incredibly easy to make this paragraph the scriptural basis for an introspective or even paranoid preparation for the Lord's Supper, so we assume that we must not come to the table as unworthy sinners lest we desecrate the sacrament (v. 27). Once at the table, we must not fail to discern the body, that is, we must fully grasp how Christ is present in the elements and how he gave his body for us (v. 29). Failure to comply with these rigorous standards will result in spiritual and even physical judgment (see v. 30). Following this line of thought, it is not difficult to understand why individuals in some Christian groups come to the Lord's Supper with great trepidation, if at all.

But Paul, ever the contextual theologian, has something quite different in mind. For him, the primary issue for the Corinthians is not "How can *I* be right with God" but "How can *we* be a loving community?" Of course, these two questions are never unrelated in Paul. Even the phrase "discerning the body" has both christological and communal meanings. In light of Paul's use of the words of institution (vv. 23–26), "discerning the body" must refer to an acceptance of Christ's death as a loving act of atonement. And it is the discernment of this sacrificial body that makes a second kind of discernment possible, a recognition of and participation in the body as community. As individuals whose bodies are linked with Christ (6:15), we are also linked with one another (12:12–13). This communal body is unique; it is wary of the world's standards and the word's offers of fellowship (10:17–21; cf. 5:1–12). It values the gifts of all its members, even those that are typically taken for granted (12:14–27). The body of Christ as community defies elitism and social stratification. In this instance, "discerning the body" would mean that a group of believers has been so changed by the radical love of Jesus Christ that the old barriers between rich and poor have disappeared.

This is much more of a corporate call to examination than an individual one. Our passage, along with the entire letter, would have been read during worship. Paul thus makes the issue of social stratification painfully communal, and surely he expects the community to make some judgment on the matter (as in 5:1–8). The community must examine itself to avoid God's discipline and even potential condemnation (11:31–32), and certain individuals will probably need to be warned. It is in the context of the community's inability to be the body that Paul makes his strange (to us) comment about sickness and death in the Corinthian church (v. 30). We must carefully note, however, that he does not say that these ailments are God's way of punishing individuals who have sinned (cf. John 9:1–3). Rather, he is making an observation about the health of the corporate body. Paul, like many Jews of his day, saw a relationship between spiritual and physical wellness (see Mark 2:1–12). If the body as community is sick, is it any wonder that individual members of this body are also sick?

Paul concludes this section with specific instructions about the observance of the Lord's Supper (vv. 33–34). He has a way of alluding to the community as family at the most opportune times (see 6:6). When brothers and sisters come together for a meal, they wait for one another (v. 33). So it is with the family of Christ at the Lord's Supper. I have always thought that Paul's reference to hunger as an explanation for the dining problems at Corinth (v. 34) is a subtle way of allowing the rich to save face. Everyone in the community might get hungry before the meal, and eating a bit at home to avoid a feeding frenzy is good advice for all.

But Paul knows full well that the real problem is the behavior of the rich. Perhaps this more general advice, coming as it does near the end of the section, is Paul's way of inviting the poor and rich to come together again, although he is certainly not negating what he has previously said. Nor is Paul finished with this issue. The fact that it will later be the topic of a face-to-face discussion (v. 34) is a clear signal about the importance of what Paul has said.

Here is the irony: it is in the act of worship that should most clearly communicate Christ's love that the Corinthian church displays its disunity. Yet Paul is alert enough as a pastor to know how to use this context to his (and the community's) advantage. By reminding them that what they *say* is inconsistent with what they *do*, he can powerfully challenge divisive class distinctions. The words of institution lie at the heart of the gospel message, a message the Corinthians need to remember if they are to be the community God wants them to be.

Paul's Words for the Contemporary Community

Tell Me the Old, Old Story

Of all the options available, Paul chooses to respond to this problem in the Corinthian church, at least initially, by telling a story. It's a natural response, of course, because he is teaching the Corinthians with the very words of institution they abuse. But what is interesting for our purposes is the way Paul assumes that this condensation of the larger gospel story will be authoritative and unifying. Paul assumes what is often not the case in our world or even in our Christian communities: that truth is singular, that there is a comprehensive story out there that explains all our individual stories and gives life meaning.

Our world is increasingly labeled *postmodern*.[8] The word *postmodernism* is a slippery and perhaps overused term, but one can begin to grasp its meaning by thinking about how and why contemporary culture rejects some of the basic assumptions of what has been called the "modern" world. Modernism, emerging out of the Enlightenment and built upon the scientific method and philosophy of Immanuel Kant, assumed that its comprehensive descriptions of reality, those truths or stories that are now called "metanarratives," were trustworthy. But why, ask the postmodern thinkers, should they be trusted? Anyone can see that there are *competing* metanarratives in the world (capitalism, Marxism, democracy, scientific truth, Christianity, and so on). Which one is right? And haven't some of the metanarratives proven incapable of fulfilling their claims: free-market capitalism has failed to eliminate poverty, and communism has not liberated the proletariat. Metanarratives, far from being universal, assume certain points of view that empower some and are unjust to others.[9] And hasn't science itself, with its quantum mechanics and theories about chaos, come to accept that truth is plural rather than singular?

One of the most helpful ways of entering into dialogue with the postmodern is to listen to artists, those creative souls who are often incredibly prophetic about the mood or direction of a culture. What do the dissonant building materials and asymmetrical shapes in contemporary architecture (for example, at the Guggenheim Museum in Bilbao, Spain) tell us about our world? What are we to make of the ugly and offensive in the visual and plastic arts (for example, the work of Andres Serrano and Robert Mapplethorpe and, of more recent notoriety, Chris Ofili's sculpture of the Virgin Mary with an exposed breast made of elephant dung)? What message should we as Christians hear in the often violent, narcissistic, and infantile lyrics of grunge, rap, and teenybopper music?

Of the many possible examples in popular music, surely the most transparent of the contemporary arts, is Sheryl Crow's song, "All I Wanna Do." It fascinates me because of what it communicates about hopelessness and isolation. It's a haunting piece, with dissonant accompaniment and verses that are spoken rather than sung, a sort of poor-white-trash country/rap. The narrative's setting is a bar in Los Angeles, and the singer is telling of her day's experience. She's met a man named "Billy or Mac or Buddy," and they have spent the day drinking beer and occasionally watching "the good people of the world" at a nearby car wash attempting to bring order to the world by washing their "Datsuns and Buicks." As day moves into night, the narrator claims to enjoy her buzz, while Billy spends his time in meaningless activity: peeling labels from bottles, lighting matches and letting them burn down to his fingers, and spinning bottles on the barroom floor. Breaking into a soulful melody for the chorus, the narrator expresses her highest aspirations: life is nothing more than a lonely attempt to "have some fun."

This song is obviously an expression of individualism gone to seed, but one that can find no ultimate meaning in either the world's work-a-day pursuits or its own quest for "fun." The present is intensified but also boring, and the piece exudes cynicism. The mood here is far different from romantic literature where an incompatibility with the world often leads to an emphasis upon personal relationships. In Matthew Arnold's "Dover Beach," written a century earlier, at least the depressed poet can muster enough courage to entreat his partner, "Ah, love, let us be true to one another!" In Crow's ballad one sees only joyless autonomy borne of a rejection of the promises of the modern world. Crow's artistry is a window on our postmodern culture because it evokes the experience of living apart from any sense of ultimate truth, without a metanarrative.

Paul's strategy in addressing the Corinthians is important for the contemporary church because it reminds us, especially as we face a postmodern world, that Christian community must be bound and shaped by a common story. On one level this means that a congregation must be what Robert Bellah calls a "community of memory,"[10] a group of people held together by a common past that is faithfully recounted. Although this is not an explicit concern in the present passage, in a real sense it is always part of Paul's agenda. The very fact that he writes letters to these churches shows his intense concern to remind people who they are, to give them a common identity. A healthy Christian community intentionally retells key events in its story: the fire that destroyed the church and its visionary response to the crisis; the church's long relationship with a certain mission project; an important church leader and how she modeled the faith for the youth of the community. (In light of all the problems at Corinth, one wonders what events they would recount in the telling of their story!) And the community relates its story in various contexts, from the pulpit, in the classroom, in small groups, and in coffee-hour conversations, so that new members can be assimilated into the tradition and the story itself molded in positive ways. In his classic *Congregation: Stories and Structures*, James Hopewell contends that the rich and varied stories of individual congregations can be classified according to four common narrative types: comic, romantic, tragic, and ironic.[11] The astute congregational "reader" will be able to discern the story's type or combination of types and thus envision how both the church's plot and its characterization might be enriched.

But Paul is asserting far more than the need for each community to know its particular story. If such were the sole basis for community, it would be very easy to manipulate the group by shaping the story in narrow or self-serving ways. The apostle is declaring that Christian community must have its origin in the metanarrative of Jesus Christ, in the truth about the One who came and gave his body so that we might be the body. These words of institution remind the Corinthians what ultimately links them together: the gospel story of Christ's sacrificial love. The remembering that the Corinthians are commanded to do is a corporate act; together they recall what Christ has done for them and how that story affects their relationships with one another. And the story of Jesus Christ is not a mere local truth that creates a tribal mentality. Paul asserts that every Christian, indeed all of creation (Romans 8:18–25), submits to the truth of the cross. Just as this story unites rich and poor in Corinth, so it unites the Corinthians with other churches that might seem impossibly different (see Romans 16:1–23, written from Corinth as Paul anticipates bringing the gentile churches' offering to the Jewish Christians in Jerusalem). Paul is clearly denying the basic postmodern assertion that all truth is relative. This story unites individual communities and Christians in all times and all places. It is worth remembering!

It is essential that we try to discern how postmodernism has affected contemporary Christian community and how Paul's words speak to this influence. Of the many possibilities, let me suggest three interrelated ways of framing the issue. First of all, Paul rejects the all too common assumption of mainstream churches that in order to be inclusive we must sacrifice our Christology. Not only is the story of Jesus Christ as presented in the words of institution inviolable, it is also precisely this message of the cross that guarantees the inclusion of all, even, as in the case of the Corinthian church, class groups that society would separate.

Second, we need to be aware of how the Christian metanarrative affirmed so powerfully by Paul defines us as community relative to the world. Claiming to possess an authoritative story puts us at odds with our postmodernist environment, but it can also make our communities more attractive. In the 1960s and 1970s people talked about the post-*Christian* world, describing the church's loss of authority to secularism. In a post-Christian world, Christianity is suspect; in a post*modern* world, *all* claims to universal truth are questioned. Postmodernism levels the ideological playing field. More important, I think, postmodernism creates a yearning for community. In a world without universal truths, the end result is the desperate individualism depicted so powerfully in Crow's ballad. But for how long can the quest for individual truth endure? If the woman portrayed by Crow has already grasped the emptiness of both the work-a-day world and its polar opposite, the day spent at the bar, surely her declared quest for "fun," whatever that means, must be seen as ironic. Perhaps authentic community is not so passé after all. It seems obvious to me that the nature of community and how it is shaped by a metanarrative is one place where dialogue between Christianity and our postmodern world can begin.

Finally, and perhaps most important, Paul is adamant that as Christians we must not act as if we were isolated individuals in the world when in reality we are members of a larger community joined together by God's love. The words of institution communicate both what we are and what we long to be. Implicit in this condensation of the gospel story is the Pauline indicative/imperative we have seen so often before: Christ has given his body; therefore, we must be his body. There must be a clear grasp of the temporal dissonance in the Christian life. The very fact that we proclaim Christ's death "until he comes" (v. 26) indicates that he has not yet come in a final sense. At times our local Christian community might look a little too much like Corinth. But the broken-ness and absence of final victory we see in the world and even in the church is not an indication that truth fails to exist or that God is not leading us into community. We are called upon to discern the body. Taking the elements of communion, we express our resounding yes to the gift of salvation in Jesus Christ and our pledge to rid ourselves of the barriers that might divide us: class differences, gender and racial divisions, personal conflict, and even our self-serving theologies. And in the already/not yet of the Christian life there is a clear sense that community is something we already experience, even as we strive to be more fully what we already are in Christ.

Neither Rich Nor Poor

First Corinthians 11:17–34 illustrates well a central claim of what is often called ideological criticism (e.g., the hermeneutic of feminism, liberation theology, and so on): that the social location of the interpreter determines how a biblical passage will be applied. I cannot presume to know how members of a base Christian community in Lima, Peru, would use this passage, although it is hard to imagine that societal tensions between rich and poor would not express themselves in powerful ways. More important, while in terms of our role in the global Christian community knowing their interpretation would be very helpful, it would not necessarily make that interpretation relevant to the particular community issues confronting my world. By necessity I address the world I know and inhabit, a world of American middle-class Christians who attend churches in mainstream denominations, we who have become extremely comfortable with the materialism of our lives and who, by standards in other parts of this planet, could rightly be called wealthy.

To us, the rigid class distinctions at Corinth seem almost unimaginable, especially when they serve to exclude the poor from consuming food, something to which we consider everyone to have an essential right. The situation at their gatherings would be roughly equivalent to that of a church potluck at which only half of those present go through the line. Our presuppositions about equality in American society make the Corinthians' behavior appear odd and make Paul's reaction appear less than radical. We look around us and perceive (rightly or not) a large middle class of people who have roughly the same income and social standing. We assume that in our democratic world the rights and opportunities of all are guaranteed by the Constitution. And the rich Corinthians' stinginess seems all the more foreign when compared with our common American ideals of neighborliness and hospitality. What red-blooded American (let alone Christian) would not respond as Paul did? Perhaps this is the reason it has been so easy to emphasize the sacramental aspects of this passage while ignoring its communal teachings; to us, Paul's defense of the poor at Corinth seems obvious, and the issue of class distinctions themselves passé.

Yet there is a sense in which Paul's imperative in this passage is radical for us. It has less to do with overt class distinctions, however, than with the sometimes subtle ways American assumptions about material things affect Christian community. When I ask church groups, "How does wealth affect your choice of friends in the church?" or "Are church leaders selected on the basis of their financial status?" the furtive glances communicate what is usually confirmed in private: that Christian communities can have the same economic pecking order as American society at large. What at first seems to be a homogeneous middle-class community might well be a church composed of several exclusive groups that distinguish among themselves on the basis of relatively small economic differences. Of all the barriers to community addressed in 1 Corinthians, I have found that this is the one contemporary American Christians have the greatest difficulty discussing openly.

During the early and middle 1980s, my involvement in our seminary's rural ministry program brought me face-to-face with numerous families that had been victimized by the rural crisis. Because of extremely depressed land and commodity prices, people who had been successful lost farms whose sod had first been tilled by their great grandparents. In many cases, the anguish of losing the family farm was compounded by a double revelation concerning their church communities. These former paragons of financial success discovered, sometimes for the first time, not only that their standing in the community was linked to their wealth but also that this standing, like their wealth, could be *lost*. People who had never questioned why they were considered pillars of the church suddenly found themselves less popular, less spoken to, and less often invited to assume positions of leadership.

Those who are unacquainted with the communal devastation caused by the farm crisis might read Jane Smiley's classic *A Thousand Acres*, a novel about the painful disintegration of one farm family unable to free itself from its lust for land. Like most good novels it is hyperbolic in places—in one scene a father and son have a fistfight at a church potluck dinner! But what is perhaps most helpful for our purposes is the way Smiley's story illustrates how utterly helpless the church can be when confronted with the changing economic status of its members. When Ginny, the dutiful elder daughter, tries to find help for her increasingly dysfunctional family, she seeks the counsel of her pastor, the Reverend Henry Dodge, believing that his office "promised a patience and capaciousness of understanding" she desperately needs. She is sorely disappointed. Arriving unannounced, Ginny finds Henry Dodge's cluttered and uninviting office open but not occupied; he's out back mowing the lawn. The phone rings and goes unanswered. When Reverend Dodge does appear, he is sweaty and trite and easily distracted. Ginny's reaction is to flee not only the incompetence of this pastor who is "too much himself, too small for his position, too anxious to fit in to our community, too sweaty and dirty and casual and unwise," but also, by implication, a church that has no capacity to deal with anything but financial success.[12]

Though our class distinctions might be more discreetly expressed than those of the Corinthians, Paul's words obviously are for us as well: discerning the body means rejecting what the world affirms about the relationship between wealth and status. In Christian community we neither humiliate people because they have nothing (11:22), nor honor others simply because they have much. If indeed our existence as a body is grounded in the loving sacrifice of Christ's body, then this new covenant (v. 25) rejects old ways of evaluating an individual's worth and place in the community. As Paul puts it in the next chapter, divisions based upon race and class disappear in the oneness of Christ's body: "For in the one Spirit we were all baptized into one body—Jews or Greeks, slaves or free" (12:13).

Of course, Paul rejects other human means of granting or withholding status as well. We have already discussed how men and women are united in ministry; compare the baptismal formula in 12:13, above, with the fuller one in Galatians 3:27–28. Also in 1 Corinthians, Paul briefly alludes (through his discussion of "boasting," especially in chapter 2; 3:21; and 4:7) to something that is a major issue elsewhere: that we can gain status before neither God nor our fellow human beings by accomplishing "works of the law" (Galatians 2:16; 3:10–14; Romans 3:27–28). Translated into the contemporary American vernacular, this means that our own achievements, whether occupational or financial or intellectual or even religious, cannot make us right with God; nor do they empower us in the Christian community. Surely a community defined by grace rather than by what we have or what we do is as countercultural for us as Paul's vision of the church is for his world. Only in this new kind of gathering is it possible for a Pharisee, a rich entrepreneur, a former slave, a divorced woman, and a Roman soldier to eat the Lord's Supper together.

But there is another way in which Paul's message is disturbing for us. The Corinthian church is the only show in town for believers, and so poor and rich Christians worship together by necessity. We, on the other hand, may already be making a decision to avoid the poor simply by choosing a particular congregation or denomination. The path of least resistance leads us to people who are like ourselves. In any given city and within the same denomination, it is common to find a blue-collar church, a professional church, and a university church. Even denominations tend to assume certain economic personalities. It could be argued that the poor avoid the rich as much as vice versa, but the economic exclusiveness of many congregations means that the poor never have the choices the rich do. Our assumption that the issues in 1 Corinthians 11:17–34 are passé indicates just how far we have removed ourselves from the poor.

At what point does our desire to be part of a Christian community that makes us feel safe and comfortable become a problem? While it may be easy to love distant poor people, the real test emerges in the definition of our mission to those who live within the shadow of our church steeples. A friend of mine recalls a question posed by the chair of his church's evangelism committee. "Who," he had the honesty to ask his committee, "do we *not* want in our church?"[13] Although seldom explicitly voiced, this is the question that determines for so many churches whether they will serve all within a given region (and thus be a "community" church) or whether they will be defined by class.

Why is it important that rich and poor people rub shoulders in the same community? The larger New Testament witness gives several reasons, all of which challenge the first-century status quo. In the Gospels, Jesus makes it clear that his message of compassion is especially for the poor (Luke 4:18–19; 6:20–21). Also important is the way more wealthy Christians are encouraged to share materially with the poor, often in Christian community that is defined as family and stands in contradistinction to the world (see Acts 2:42–47; 6:1–6, and especially Mark 10:28–31). Especially interesting is the way the New Testament writers assume that the rich in the community need the reality check offered by their less materially blessed sisters and brothers. As the author of 1 Timothy puts it: "But those who want to be rich fall into temptation and are trapped by many senseless and harmful desires that plunge people into ruin and destruction" (1 Timothy 6:9; see also vv. 10, 17–19). James pointedly warns the church against treating the rich better than they treat the poor (2:1–10) and is clear about the dangers associated with material riches (1:9–11; 5:1–5).

Paul asserts that poor and rich need each other. The poor need the material things others in the community can share. This principle is illustrated powerfully in the larger church by Paul's collection for the poor in Jerusalem (see 2 Corinthians 8–9) and by the support he himself received (Philippians 4:15–16). The presence of the disenfranchised and poor in the community is a clear reminder for both the rich and the poor that what we have in Christ does not come through human achievement (1 Corinthians 1:28–31). And 1 Corinthians 12 reminds us that the community cannot be the body of Christ without its diverse parts (vv. 12–31); the gifts of all are necessary.

The rationale for an inclusive community that is emphasized in 1 Corinthians 11:17–34 is the cross of Jesus Christ; the message is communicated with stark power in the words of institution. How does remembering that Christ gave his body for us (v. 24) affect the way we live in community? How does the new covenant in Christ's blood shape us communally? The most basic answer, of course, is that we have been changed and empowered by the self-giving love of the cross; we are a people who in our relationships with one another "proclaim the Lord's death until he comes" (v. 26). We become Christ's body, new creations (2 Corinthians 5:17) who are able to love those whom the world tells us to avoid. As Paul so succinctly affirms in the reversal that lies at the heart of our new perception of those around us: "For you know the generous act of our Lord Jesus Christ, that though he was rich, yet for your sakes he became poor, so that by his poverty you might become rich" (2 Corinthians 8:9).

This also means that the old distinctions between rich and poor begin to disintegrate, as do those that divide Jews and Gentiles, slaves and free, and men and women in Paul's churches (1 Corinthians 12:13; Galatians 3:28). If all are a new creation, if all were poor but have become rich in Christ, and if all practice the love they see in the cross, then Christian community will threaten class distinctions. I cannot agree with those who see the equality Paul advocates as one that is only "in Christ" and has no concrete implications for status and power in the community. Gerd Theissen, for instance, labels Paul's strategy in our passage "love patriarchalism," in which the different classes express "respect and love"[14] toward one another, but do not challenge social stratification. It is true that Paul does not speak of communal sharing as clearly as Luke does when he describes the early church at Jerusalem (Acts 2:43–47). And certainly Paul's vision for social change has been affected by his assumption that Christ will return soon (1 Corinthians 7:25–31). But there is no doubt that the class unity Paul advocates impacts community in concrete and radical ways. For rich and poor to dine at the same table, eating the body and blood that unites them, is already a declaration of freedom from the world's standards, one that would by necessity change how these groups relate elsewhere in the community. At the very least Paul's words have implications for the stewardship of material things. Without being as prescriptive as we might like him to be, Paul makes it clear in his collection speech in 2 Corinthians that a sharing of economic resources is part of his vision for the community: "I do not mean that there should be relief for others and pressure on you, but it is a question of a fair balance between your present abundance and their need, so that their abundance may be for your need, in order that there may be a fair balance" (8:13–14).

The several references in 1 Corinthians to communal problems that grow out of class distinctions indicate that the issue was both common and stubborn. Community as the body of Christ was a frontal attack on the first-century status quo. Although social stratification manifests itself differently in our world, the gospel Paul preaches is radical for us as well. It is important to remind ourselves just how difficult it may be to build a community where status is not linked to wealth or achievement, and class differences begin to disappear. As in any situation where the church stands in direct opposition to the world, we as individual disciples must recognize how much we need the support of the larger group. Even though we have been transformed in Christ, it is impossible to fight these battles on our own. Perhaps the place to begin is with a communal self-examination of the sort Paul prescribes in 11:27–32. Have we as individual communities discerned the body? Or have we stood in the way of a proclamation meant for all people? It is quite possible that some congregations need to be called to a heartfelt repentance as people "answerable for the body and blood of the Lord" (v. 27). Paul's words are a powerful reality check for those who somehow think they can enjoy the benefits of the body and blood that have been given for us without also living as changed people in a community open to all.

Community
and Spiritual Gifts

1 Corinthians 12–14

The fact that mainstream churches often ignore precisely the biblical passages about community they most need to hear is a sad irony, but one that does follow a certain logic; it is always easiest to avoid the message that issues the clearest and most radical challenge to our communal status quo. In our interpretation of 1 Corinthians 12–14, this avoidance takes several forms. Our paranoia about speaking in tongues tempts us to misunderstand what Paul says about it and allows us to devalue generally the role of spiritual gifts in the community. Our wariness of these gifts is perhaps the best explanation for the way we separate chapter 13 from its context, making it an ode to individual and sometimes romantic love rather than a foundational statement about the practice of love in community. Just as commonly, we are easily convinced that because Paul is critiquing people who are zealous for spiritual gifts, his words have little relevance for those of us who are more reserved about this spiritual empowerment. We ignore what is implicit in his message for people who are quite unlike the Corinthians.

Once again, Paul is called upon to combat a significant barrier to community in the Corinthian church. This barrier expresses itself in several ways, but all are directly related to the Corinthians' use of speaking in tongues during corporate worship. Perhaps most essential is the way their desire for this particular gift limits the expression of spiritual gifts in the church. For the first time in this letter, Paul argues at length for the value of diversity within Christian community (chapter 12). Paul also deals with the effect speaking in tongues has had on worship and therefore community at Corinth. He insists that if worship is to benefit all those who are gathered, it must be intelligible and orderly (chapter

129

14). Finally, and perhaps most subtly, Paul discusses the tension between church members at Corinth that is based on the way spiritual gifts are valued. All gifts are important, Paul asserts (12:20–25), and their use must be governed by Christian love (chapter 13). Gifts are intended to build up the community, not divide it. This section of 1 Corinthians continues to be highly relevant for mainline churches, not only in terms of what it says about community generally, but also because of what it tells us about the use and abuse of spiritual gifts.

1 Corinthians 12

Because Paul is responding to their inquiry ("now concerning"; cf. 7:1, 8:1), the Corinthians know what the essential issue is, and so his strategy to delay talking explicitly about the use of tongues in worship makes good rhetorical sense. Before he makes his pronouncement about how tongues should be used (chapter 14), Paul is very careful to give a theological rationale for the use of spiritual gifts in community: the Spirit gives all believers gifts that build up the body of Christ (chapter 12), and all gifts are governed by Christian love (chapter 13). Although this is the most extensive discussion of empowerment through the Spirit in 1 Corinthians, it is not the first. In 2:1–3:4 Paul issues a biting criticism of the Corinthians' spiritual maturity. Here his words are more even-tempered (at least until the end of chapter 14), but in both cases it is obvious that Paul and the Corinthians are at odds in terms of how the Spirit should manifest itself in the Christian life.

Paul begins with a clear warning that is important for our new-age attitudes as well: not all spirituality is Christian spirituality (12:1–3). It is quite possible to be empowered by alien spirits (see 10:20) that lead to idolatry and rejection of Jesus (12:2–3), as the Corinthians know by experience. Conversely, and this is Paul's main point in the first paragraph of chapter 12, the lived confession that Jesus is Lord can be made only by those who have received the Holy Spirit (v. 3). A believer's relationship with Jesus Christ is the most basic indicator of the presence and empowerment of the Spirit.

Does this response by the apostle indicate that some at Corinth are openly charging that fellow church members do not possess the Holy Spirit? Probably not, but Paul's words are a necessary reminder to those who imply that very thing by failing to recognize the diverse gifts of the Spirit. The Holy Spirit indwells *all* Christians, and the resulting spiritual gifts are necessary "for the common good" (12:7), or, as Paul repeatedly puts it in chapter 14, for the building up of the church (14:4–5, 12, 26). One of the paradoxes of the Corinthian church is that they fail to understand unity at various communal levels, but here, when it comes to spiritual gifts, they fail to understand diversity. Their narrowness forces Paul to make his clearest statement in all of his letters about the relationship between the one and the many in community, or, as he puts it in his well-known metaphor, the relationship between the body and the parts (12:12–30).

Certainly Paul's mention of the three members of the Trinity in 12:4–6 (Spirit, v. 4; Lord, v. 5; God, v. 6) is a subtle reminder that the concept of the one and the many exists mysteriously in the Godhead itself. More obvious is the way he combats prideful attitudes concerning spiritual empowerment by clearly naming the source and purpose of that empowerment. The same Lord, God, and Spirit (Spirit is used in vv. 7–13 to stand for all the members of the Trinity) is the author of all gifts (vv. 4–11). And Paul makes it clear that these are gifts (*charismata*, vv. 4–11), intentionally shifting his terminology from the word *pneumatikos* in verse 1, a more generic term meaning "spiritual things" or "spiritual people." (The Corinthians apparently preferred the word *pneumatikos* [see 14:12]; unfortunately the NRSV also translates this term as "spiritual gifts".) Christians' spiritual empowerment has been *given* (see the verb form in vv. 7–8). The Spirit *activates* it (v. 11; cf. v. 6). Gifts are allotted as the Spirit *chooses* (v. 11). Those who might be tempted to use spiritual empowerment as a personal toy are reminded that it is for service (v. 5). The spiritual gifts we receive through the Holy Spirit are very much like the salvation we receive in Christ: they are purely of grace and say nothing about our own achievement or status.

This Holy Spirit, the Spirit working in all believers, issues an incredible variety of gifts for the building up of the community. The list Paul offers in vv. 8–10 is an illustration of the possibilities (cf. vv. 27–30; Romans 12:6–8; and Ephesians 4:11–13; see also the list of the fruit of the Spirit in Galatians 5:22). Astute Corinthian hearers will recognize that Paul includes their preferred gifts (wisdom, knowledge [v. 8], and tongues [v. 10]), but also that he names gifts less prized in the community, such as faith, healing (v. 9), working of miracles, prophecy, discernment of spirits, and interpretation of tongues (v. 10). And certainly they will understand that the placement of the gift of tongues near the end of the list, here and in verses 27–30, is no accident. Paul's words are an implicit criticism of the homogeneity of gifts at Corinth, of a narrowness that amounts to a denial of the creative work of the Spirit.

But even more is at stake. Building on his statement that the many gifts of the Spirit are "for the common good" (v. 7), Paul introduces a vivid metaphor of the body and the parts to affirm the need for diversity in the community (vv. 14–26). He certainly didn't invent this image, but its common use in the first century would make it a useful teaching device for the Corinthians. Rhetoricians, politicians, and storytellers of Paul's day often speak about the relationship between the body and the parts, sometimes referring to the same organs Paul mentions.[1] Typically the metaphor is employed for political purposes, to squelch criticism of the state especially by putting the lower classes in their place.[2] In the tale by Menenius Agrippa (fifth century B.C.E.), for instance, a story of the rebellion of certain parts of the body (hands, mouth, and teeth) against the belly is used to argue against peasant unrest.[3]

As in this literature, Paul speaks of the unity of the parts for the good of the body. The body is "one" (vv. 12–13, 20). Believers who are "Jews or Greeks, slaves or free" become one body through the one Spirit (v. 13).[4] It is impossible to read Paul's use of the metaphor in verses 14–26 without concluding that the body has an important function and that the individual parts must contribute to this corporate good. With the Corinthian community obviously in mind, Paul says that there should be no "dissension" (*schisma*, v. 25; see also 1:10; 11:18) in the body and that the members should care for one another and suffer and rejoice together (vv. 25–26). As we shall see in chapter 14, those who disrupt worship and elevate their own spiritual status through the gift of speaking in tongues need to be reminded again of the oneness of the body.

Thus, on the one hand Paul's use of the metaphor is consistent with its use earlier in the letter (see 10:17 and 11:29) and consistent with its typical function in the first-century world. In Jesus Christ the individual is subservient to the body of believers. But Paul's metaphor unexpectedly moves in the opposite direction as well. In two carefully composed parallel sections (vv. 14–19 and 20–26), the main point of Paul's rendering of the metaphor is immediately obvious: a *diversity* of parts is absolutely essential for the proper functioning of the body. The arguments for secession spoken by the personified foot (v. 15) and ear (v. 16) are not allowed to stand. Only when the body has a full range of functioning parts can it operate as a body (v. 17). In fact, God intended this variety; he "chose" such an arrangement of parts (v. 18). Paul is clearly challenging any tendency in the Corinthian church to seek only certain spiritual gifts and thus limit the diversity of gifts necessary for a healthy community.

The specific problem at Corinth is perhaps even more directly targeted in the next section (vv. 20–26), where the metaphor emphasizes tensions between so-called superior and inferior parts. The personified eye cannot declare that it has no need of the lowly hand, nor can the head question the importance of the feet (v. 21). Pushing this image even farther, Paul points out the ironic relationship between the weak and strong and the unrespectable and respectable members (vv. 22–24). The apparently weaker members (the internal organs?) are actually the least dispensable (v. 22), while the less respectable members (the sexual organs?) are given greater respect (vv. 23–24), and all of this is according to God's plan (v. 24). Diversity in the body manifests itself as interdependence among the parts. In contrast to the typical use of the metaphor in the Greco-Roman world, Paul assumes that members of various "ranks" need (vv. 21–22) and take care of one another (vv. 23–26). The apostle's words are a not-so-subtle warning to those among the Corinthians who consider themselves superior because they speak in tongues. The spiritual gifts and those who practice them are inescapably linked, like the parts of a human body, and only when these diverse members live interdependently will the community be whole.

Paul concludes this chapter with a crystal-clear application (vv. 27–30) for those who may have somehow missed his point. He again lists the varied spiritual gifts that God has appointed in the church, most certainly getting the attention of the Corinthians by putting tongues at the end (v. 28; the ranking of the first three items corresponds to their chronological appearance in the early church). Paul then asks a series of rhetorical questions that demand (through the use of the word *mē*) a negative answer (vv. 29–30). Are all Christians prophets? Are all miracle workers? Do all speak in tongues? Of course not! The Holy Spirit's gifts are diverse beyond imagining, and all build up the body of Christ (v. 27). Paul's final words about the "greater gifts" and the "more excellent way" (v. 31) are a transition to the discussion in chapters 13 and 14. Although they are somewhat confusing at this point, they do not contradict what he has just affirmed about the importance of varied gifts in the community, as we shall see in the following sections.

And so the community, at least in terms of how it uses its spiritual gifts, is like a body. But throughout this letter, and especially in chapter 12, Paul also assumes that the community is the body *of Christ* (vv. 12, 27). It is fascinating to see how easily Paul moves between *body* as a metaphor that describes the function of community and *body* of Christ as a way of speaking about the nature of the community in relationship to Christ. Paul hints at this in chapter 6, where he tells us that the bodies of individual Christians are members (*mele*, the same word that is translated "part" or "member" in chapter 12) of Christ (v. 15). We experience a mystical union with Christ that even makes our physical bodies temples of the Holy Spirit (6:17, 19; cf. 3:16). In 10:17, foreshadowing the use of the metaphor in chapter 12, Paul emphasizes the unity of the community to this divisive church by saying that the many are one body. But standing alongside this metaphor, and more pivotal than it (at least in chapter 10), is Paul's insistence that the community is a sharing (*koinōnia*, 10:16) in the body of Christ. The church stands in rela-

Christ and represents him in the world, making it a unique
s with pagan fellowship (10:20–21). A similar twofold use of
d in chapter 11. Those who fail to discern the body in the
le Lord's Supper incur judgment (11:29). On the one hand,
this is a warning to those who ignore the imperative that all parts of the
community as body (in this case, rich and poor) must live in unity. On
the other hand, Paul is clearly reminding the Corinthians that they are
the body of Christ, born of his loving work on the cross.

Although it is easy for us to separate these two functions of the term
body in 1 Corinthians, it is obvious, especially in chapter 12, that Paul
sees them as intertwined. At times he clearly uses *body* as an analogy
for both the one and the many, a common illustration (vv. 14–26). But
what does the apostle intend to communicate when he asserts that just
as the body is both one and many, "so it is with Christ" (v. 12)? Is he trying to say that diversity is an essential part of Christ's nature? Or is *body*
here simply shorthand for *body of Christ* or *church*? In verse 27 we read
Paul's declaration that the Corinthians are the body of Christ. Coming
as it does after a discussion of the value of diverse parts of the body
(vv. 12–26) and before a statement about the importance of the various
individual spiritual gifts (vv. 27–30), how do you think the declaration
is heard by the Corinthians? Obviously they are reminded again that
they stand in relationship to Christ, having their origin and empowerment in the one who gave his body on the cross. But given the immediate literary context, I think Paul is also forcing them to consider how
their diverse spiritual gifts represent Christ in the church and world.
They become the varied parts of Christ's body, his hands and feet, his
eyes and ears, to act in love (chapter 13) and service (12:5) on his behalf.
Thus *body* as metaphor for the one and the many and *body* as a term
indicating Christ's claim upon us meld into one, much as they do in
Ephesians and Colossians, where Christ is pictured as the head of the
body and the image takes on its most sophisticated form (Ephesians
4:15–16; Colossians 1:15–20).

1 Corinthians 13

It needs to be stated at the outset that love is not one of the "greater
gifts" Paul encourages the Corinthians to strive for in 12:31; the apostle will address the issue of the ranking of spiritual gifts in chapter 14.
Rather, by calling it a "more excellent way" (12:31), Paul both distinguishes love from spiritual gifts altogether and asserts that it is something all Christians should practice as they use their gifts. Love is more
basic in the Christian life than spiritual gifts; it governs the use of those

gifts and indeed all relations in Christian community. Chapter 13 and the practice of love speak directly to the problem Paul is addressing here: the abuse of spiritual gifts during worship. But Paul's words in the chapter also form the spiritual center of the entire letter, his most comprehensive answer to the community problems the Corinthians are experiencing. Interestingly, Paul describes the practice of Christian love in every issue he addresses, although he does not commonly use the word itself, in either noun or verb form (see 2:9; 4:21; 8:3; 16:14, 24 and especially 8:1: "Knowledge puffs up, but love builds up"). It's almost as if the apostle has intentionally curtailed its use until now, waiting so he can spring upon his audience this communal punch line, doubly powerful because of its rhetorical sophistication.

Each of the three paragraphs in chapter 13 has a unique structure, yet all are highly poetic, employing both figurative language and rhythm.[5] Paul grabs the Corinthians' attention in 13:1–3 by presenting three sentences of parallel structure and similar yet crescendoing meaning: if I have a valued gift or do a good deed, but don't have love, it is meaningless. The gifts the Corinthians pursue, speaking in tongues of mortals (a reference to their infatuation with gifted speakers [cf. 1:18–31]?) and of angels (cf. chapter 14),[6] are like the empty sounds of pagan worship (gongs and cymbals) if they do not grow out of love (13:1). Upping the ante, Paul says that even the gifts *he* is promoting as the superior ones, prophecy (14:1, 3, 5, and so on) and faith (12:9; 13:13), amount to nothing if they are not practiced in love (v. 2). Finally, Paul makes a third and yet more hyperbolic statement: actions that represent the extreme in Christian sacrifice, giving away one's possessions or handing over one's body (as a slave or perhaps as a martyr?), if they are not done in love, benefit nothing (v. 3). Could the Corinthians have failed to hear a point driven home so clearly? Even those gifts and activities Christians consider the best they have to offer, in the case of the Corinthians their prized ability to speak in tongues, are meaningless if they do not originate in Christ's love and express this love toward others.

For the Christian, then, love is everything. But what is love? Paul's answer in verses 4–7 is what we might expect: a response to the Corinthians' shortcomings concerning communal love. It reflects many of the misperceptions about love addressed throughout this letter. The contextual basis of Paul's description of love means it is not a comprehensive definition. In these verses he focuses narrowly on ethics, or how the Corinthians should love one another, not, at least explicitly, on Christology, or the origin of our love in Jesus Christ. As in verses 1–3, Paul's language becomes powerful through repetition, here in the cadence of repeated words and sounds that describe what love is and is not.

If the Corinthians are honest with themselves, they will most certainly hear this list that describes the function of love as an indictment. Think of the ways this divided community lacks patience and kindness (v. 4), qualities that Paul attributes to God in Romans 2:4. Love is not envious or jealous (v. 4), Paul asserts, using the same word he employs in 3:3 to describe their infantile and schismatic behavior. Nor is it boastful (v. 4), exhibiting an attitude Paul has repeatedly seen in the Corinthians (see 1:29–31; 3:21; 4:7; 5:6; Paul uses a different verb for *boast* here in 13:4, but only because he has just used his more common word, *kauchaomai*, in a nonpejorative sense in 13:3). If love is not arrogant or puffed up (v. 4), then what does the Corinthians' self-centered behavior say about the state of their community relations in Corinth (4:6, 18–19; 5:2; and especially 8:1)?

And so Paul continues, driving his point home to the Corinthians in what must seem an interminable list. Some of them *have* been "shameless" (v. 5a, "rude" in the NRSV; see 7:36 and other situations where shame is involved: 5:1–2; 6:13–20; 11:5, 22). Contrary to what Paul models (10:33), some *have* insisted on having their own way (v. 5; cf. 10:24). Paul certainly considers them thin-skinned and overly diligent at remembering ways they have been wronged (v. 5, "irritable" and "resentful" in the NRSV). With more than a bit of satire the apostle implies that they actually rejoice in injustice (v. 6, "wrongdoing" in the NRSV), while Christian love should engender communal celebration (*syngchairō*, "to rejoice together") in moral truth. In a final sentence empowered both by repetition and rich theological language, Paul reminds the Corinthians of the radical nature of the love they claim but often fail to practice: love "bears all things, believes all things, hopes all things, endures all things" (v. 7).

In addition to making these highly contextual statements about the centrality of love (vv. 1–3) and the communal function of love (vv. 4–7), Paul feels compelled to describe the enduring nature of love, again with more than just side-glances at the Corinthian church (vv. 8–13). This final paragraph also takes on a poetic form that is common in the first century but unknown to most modern readers: a type of reverse parallelism called chiasm.[7] Identifying verses 8–13 as a chiasm allows us to be conscious of the structure of this paragraph and to compare parallel parts:

   A. 13:8a ("Love never ends")
      B. 13:8b
         C. 13:9–10
            D. 13:11
         C'. 13:12
      B'. 13:13a
   A'. 13:13b ("and the greatest of these is love")

Paul's main point is that love is the bedrock of the Christian life, both now and as it will be experienced in God's eschatological future. And so it is superior to spiritual gifts, important though they may be, because they function only in the time before the end. The parallel statements at the beginning and end of this chiasm (A, A': v. 8a, v. 13b) declare the temporal superiority of love. "Love never ends," but the spiritual gifts both Paul and the Corinthians champion, prophecies, tongues, and knowledge, will be nullified (B: v. 8b, "will come to an end" in the NRSV; this word, *katargeō*, is often used by Paul to speak of God's eschatological abolishment [see 1:28; 6:13; 15:24, 26]). Both here and in the next section (C: vv. 9–10) Paul is very careful to include prophecy, his own "preferred" gift (see chapter 14), to show that he is not just squabbling about which gift is best. *All* spiritual gifts belong to this age. But of course his words are a criticism of the Corinthians' attitude toward prized gifts. Some at Corinth apparently act as if their knowledge and gift of tongues are signs of the "complete" or "perfect" (*teleion*, v. 10), indications that they are already fully experiencing God's future in their midst. In fact, these gifts are only "partial" (vv. 9–10), and God will soon bring them to an end (v. 10).

Verse 11, the center of the chiasm (D), must be interpreted within the eschatological context of the paragraph. Paul is not speaking about a maturing process; love does not somehow develop out of the spiritual gifts. Instead, the image of child and adult is another way of thinking about the partial and complete (v. 10), the enigmatic and the clear (as we shall see in v. 12). Put simply, life in the present age is different from life in the age to come, and some of the things Christians experience in the present, even good things like spiritual gifts, will be left behind. For those at Corinth who are able to hear, Paul is also making a comment about those who are so childish they prefer the temporal to the enduring (cf. 3:1–3 and Paul's reference to the Corinthians as "infants").

With verse 12 (C') clearly parallel in meaning to verses 9–10 (C), the chiasm begins its pattern of reversal. The power of this poetic structure lies in the way the second part of the parallelism is always enough unlike the first to encourage further insight in the reader. Ideas and images are nuanced. Both C and C' contrast the incompleteness of the present with the perfection of the future, with a special emphasis upon knowledge and knowing. Yet notice what C' (v. 12) adds: the use of *now* and *then* to exaggerate the difference between present and future; the striking contrast of seeing in the mirror (interestingly, a well-known commercial product of Corinth) and seeing indirectly and "face to face" (see Genesis 32:30 and Numbers 12:8 for the use of this phrase relative to God). And notice especially the last clause in verse 12, "even as I have been fully known"; Paul breaks out of the contrast between *our* present and future knowing to emphasize that God, even now, knows us fully. These words surely address the Corinthians' eschatological confusion. God's future does enter our present, but contrary to what some of them assume, such divine knowing does not mean that we are fully gifted in the present.

Verse 13a (B') contrasts the things that end (B, v. 8b: prophecy, tongues, and knowledge) with three things that do abide in the present (taking the word for "now" temporally), faith, hope, and love. But if the gifts mentioned in verse 8b also function in the present, then in what sense do these latter three "abide"? Paul often groups faith, hope, and love together in his writings (see Romans 5:1–5; Galatians 5:5–6; 1 Thessalonians 1:3; 5:8), and in the early church it was probably common to use them as a summation for a believer's relationship with Christ. Paul most certainly considers faith, hope, and love more essential than the gifts he mentions in verse 8b. Even more important, of the three things mentioned in verse 13a, only love is both a present and future reality. Love, along with faith and hope, are now present; they all abide in the sense that there are no more fundamental expressions of our new life in Christ. But love surpasses even faith and hope: faith is fulfilled when we see God face-to-face (v. 12); hope is a longing for the new age and is left behind when it actually arrives. Love is the greatest of the three (A', v. 13b) because it represents our future relationship with God.

Thus, not only does Paul describe the preeminence of love in the final paragraph of chapter 13, but he does so by critiquing the Corinthians' eschatology. None of the spiritual gifts they prize, indeed none of the gifts the community experiences, will extend into the new age. Only love endures. Paul would certainly agree that the empowerment of the Holy Spirit is a sign of God's future kingdom, but the Corinthians' cherished gifts, notably including speaking in tongues, do not prove they have already arrived. As we have seen before, the Corinthians have a tendency to become so absorbed in the newness of the faith, especially those things that bring individual freedom and empowerment, that they often ignore their everyday responsibilities in community.

1 Corinthians 14

Paul links chapter 14 with what he has previously said by reaffirming the centrality of love ("Pursue love," v. 1) and by elaborating, finally, on his odd command to "strive for the greater gifts" (12:31). The command sounds odd to us because it comes at the end of a chapter in which Paul affirms the value of all spiritual gifts. But Paul does have a hierarchy of gifts in mind. It is one that, like the gospel tradition of lifting up the lowly and thus reversing the status quo ("The last will be first" [Mark 10:31]), is meant to challenge the Corinthians' selfish understanding of gifts. Prophecy, the gift of speaking and interpreting God's word, is a "greater gift" because it is intelligible (vv. 6–12) to all and thus "builds up" the community (*oikodomeō*, vv. 4–5, 12, 17, 26), whereas speaking in tongues "builds up" the individual (v. 4). Tongues occupy the part of a human Paul calls "spirit" (v. 14), but worship should involve both spirit and mind (v. 15). In fact, gifts that employ the mind are to be preferred in community worship, where instruction is a necessity (v. 19).

We who are puzzled by tongues-speaking in our own world must attempt to understand what this gift means to the Corinthians. It may come as a surprise to us in mainstream denominations that this spiritual gift would not be devalued by educated, high-status Christians in the first-century world. As Dale Martin has shown, in Paul's time tongues are thought to be the language of angels (see 13:1). They are not gibberish; instead, they are a higher, more spiritual way of speaking and communicating with God.[8] Quoting the *Testament of Job,* the Montanists, Tertullian, Irenaeus, and even non-Christian writers, Martin illustrates just how sought-after these tongues are. Tongues-speaking expresses itself in the sphere of humanity called "spirit," which even intellectuals of that day assume to be superior to the sphere of mind.[9] Mind "is the realm of common sensibility," but spirit is that of "esoteric knowledge."[10]

This means that Paul's discussion in 14:1–25 is not simply about the tension between the intelligible and the unintelligible. It probably also reflects the tensions between groups of different social status within the community that we detected earlier in the letter. Some at Corinth, perhaps the wealthy and the well-educated, believe they have gifts that operate "in the spirit." Paul does not dispute this. In fact, he aligns himself with this group to some extent by claiming that he himself speaks in tongues more than anyone at Corinth (v. 18). But he challenges those who possess this esoteric gift by asserting that worship must never exclude gifts that operate within the sphere of the mind, which all people share. Spiritual gifts used in worship are not about an individual spiritual "high"; nor should we seek in them a status that separates us from the community. Governed by love, a gift is intended to build up the church, not the individual who has received it (v. 4).

In practical terms, this means that tongues must always be interpreted when used in worship (vv. 5, 27–28). If they are not, they become merely meaningless noise (vv. 7–11). This is an issue not just for church members, but also for outsiders who happen to be attending (vv. 20–25). On the basis of his interpretation of Isaiah 28, Paul concludes that tongues can be nothing more than a sign of destruction for unbelievers (vv. 21–22), allowing them to misinterpret Christianity as another form

of spiritual ecstasy (v. 23). Prophecy, on the other hand, can open unbelievers' hearts to God and allow them to recognize God's presence in the
community (v. 25).

It also means that tongues and their interpretation must not detract
from the orderliness of worship, as Paul conceives it (vv. 26–40). On the
basis of his understanding of the peaceful order within God (v. 33), the
apostle affirms what has become a slogan for those of us in mainline,
especially Reformed, churches: "all things are to be done decently and
in order" (v. 40). But where is the order? By our standards what Paul
suggests seems incredibly unplanned and open-ended. Everyone comes
with some material or gift to share, a hymn, a lesson, a revelation, a
tongue, or an interpretation (v. 26). As many as three tongues-speakers,
with an interpreter, can take part (vv. 27–28). And three prophecies can
be heard, with some corporate evaluation of what has been said (v. 29).
Paul's "rules" seem to be only that they must not all talk at once (v. 31)
and that all must be done to "build up" the community (v. 26; "so that
all may learn and all be encouraged" [v. 31]).

Who prints the bulletin? Who monitors what material can be brought
to the service? What if worship extends beyond an hour? These ironic
questions are important because they help us to see this section, and
indeed all of chapter 14, in a way that is not distorted by our context
and by our awkwardness around the issue of spiritual gifts. Paul does
limit the use of tongues in worship, but he does not in any way prohibit
it. What we often too narrowly see as a passage about the prohibition
of tongues is really a resounding affirmation of spiritual gifts and the
Spirit's work in worship. Worship can be creative and free *and* orderly
because the Spirit is ultimately in charge. When Paul says that "the spirits of prophets are subject to the prophets" (v. 32) he is making a statement not only about the Corinthians' ability to control their gifts (hence,
speaking in tongues is not just "ecstasy"), but also about the Spirit's control of us.

Paul's conclusion to chapter 14 indicates an intensity around this
issue that has been fairly well concealed up to this point. It should be
noted that verse 33b, "as in all the churches of the saints," goes with
verse 33a and does not begin a new sentence. Most certainly verses 34–35
are a later interpolation (cf. 2 Corinthians 6:14–7:1). They can be omit-
ted without breaking the train of thought, they are found after verse 40
in the Western tradition, and what they say about women is inconsistent with 11:2–16.[11] Once these verses are removed, verse 36 becomes a
biting satirical remark to those at Corinth who disagree with his view
of spiritual gifts (cf. the satire in 4:8–13). Paul even takes the unusual
step of calling his instructions on this matter "a command of the Lord"
(v. 37). This prescriptive tone is accentuated in the next verse by Paul's

use of a literary form called a "pronouncement of holy law," a device in which one describes a person's sin against God and then uses the same verb to indicate God's final punishment of that person: "If anyone does not recognize this, God will not recognize him" (v. 38, my translation).[12] Paul's assertive conclusion to this section indicates that the Corinthians' failure to recognize the diversity of inspired gifts and their failure to practice them in love is indeed a serious threat to community.

Paul's Words for the Contemporary Community

Through the spiritual gifts, we are empowered by the Holy Spirit to serve those within the body of Christ, especially when we come together in worship. As we have seen, these gifts are given for service (12:5), for "the common good" (12:7), and "so that the church may be built up" (14:5).[13] Of course the Spirit's presence and his shaping and empowering of believers is a clear eschatological sign. What the prophets envisioned, an end-times outpouring of the Spirit (see Ezekiel 36:22–32), was begun at Pentecost. In 1 Corinthians Paul speaks of the bestowal of the Spirit as a sure indication that God's future is present: Christians have received a long-hidden wisdom not characteristic of this age (2:6–13). Both corporately (3:16–17) and individually (6:19) we are temples in which the Holy Spirit has come to dwell, and the Holy Spirit has begun his long-awaited task of showering God's people with spiritual gifts (12:4–11).

The eschatological nature of the gifts of the Spirit is important to recognize because it lies at the heart of the community problem that Paul addresses in this section of the letter. On the one hand, Paul and the Corinthians agree that the presence of the Holy Spirit is a sign of the new age and that the gifts imparted must be taken seriously. On the other hand, the Corinthians dispute (or misunderstand) Paul's teachings about the already/not yet of the kingdom and the nature of the eschatological community. Their conflict with Paul concerning spiritual gifts is characterized by a paradoxical attraction to extremes. They pursue tongues, one of the most spectacular and visible of the gifts, assuming that it is a full experience of the new age; Paul must remind them that it is nothing compared with what they shall see (13:8–12). They selfishly ignore the diversity of gifts in their community; Paul must remind them that the love that serves all and therefore values the gifts of all is the clearest glimpse of the *eschaton*.

Here is the hard truth: our use of the spiritual gifts and the eschatology that undergirds it is even more distant from Paul's teaching than was that of the Corinthians. Like them, we are often cavalier about the diversity of spiritual gifts and their foundation in Christian love. But unlike the Corinthians, we often fail even to acknowledge that God's future has entered our present in the Holy Spirit, and thus ignore the empowerment we so desperately need. Standing as we are with one foot planted in the "not yet," the other in the "already," how might we be shaped as a community by Paul's vision of the spiritual gifts?

Polyphony

Why is a diversity of spiritual gifts important for community? The image of the body and its parts suggests a practical necessity: in order for the body to be complete, each part, limb, or organ must serve its unique function. This illustration has lost none of its power since Paul used it. In fact, we are probably much more aware than the Corinthians of the special and necessary uses of our many body parts. Obviously there are other ways to picture this relationship between the one and the many, and at times it is valuable to supplement a well-known biblical analogy. To use a mechanical theme: the engine in your car would be incapacitated by the absence of any one of a host of tiny parts. Without its modem or thousands of much smaller electrical devices, your computer would have no chance of surfing the Web. The application is clear: if a Christian community is to be whole and therefore to function properly, it needs the spiritual gifts of all its members.

But Paul's words in this section of 1 Corinthians suggest far more than the utility of diverse gifts. A careful reading of his argument points to a theological rationale as well, one that affirms diversity as a reflection of God's nature and, therefore, as a way of grasping the richness and beauty of community life. Perhaps the place to begin is the apostle's brief, almost parenthetical statement in 14:33: "for God is a God not of disorder but of peace" (*eirēnē*). Worship, with its proper use of diverse spiritual gifts, is a reflection of the person of God. Notice that Paul does not offer a contrast to disorder by describing God as "order" or "unity" or "oneness." Rather, God is a God of peace, of shalom. Peace, used in this context, refers to diverse elements working in harmony. Paul's obvious intent in this section is to make a statement about the importance of order in worship (see also v. 40), but diversity is not sacrificed to that order. Paul is affirming, especially with this statement about the nature of God, that communal diversity lies close to our theological core.

Notice also Paul's christological statements in 12:12 and 27. Even if we see Paul's use of *Christ* in verse 12 as shorthand for "the body of Christ," the church, he is certainly also making a statement about the nature of Christ. How is Paul's constant reminder that Christ's body has many members significant christologically? Does he mean to say that diversity is actually part of Christ's nature? At the very least, as we see in Galatians 3:28, Paul is saying that Christ welcomes the full diversity of humankind in his person. In verse 27 Paul tells the Corinthians that they *are* the body of Christ, upping the ante from previous paragraphs, where he simply *compares* them to a human body (vv. 14–26). I find it fascinating that Paul immediately follows this equation of Christ and community with a reminder that they are "individually members of" the body (v. 27). His point is that Christ is a body with many parts, and that these parts serve him and therefore each other in an incredible variety of ways (12:28–30). Diversity in the community is a reflection of who Christ is.

The same is true of the Holy Spirit, who chooses (12:11) to bestow not one or two good gifts, but an infinite variety for the building up of the church (12:7–11). *Spirit* is not some theological afterthought or ghostly presence, but the way Paul chooses to talk about God as empowerment, consistent with what we see elsewhere in the early church. And notice how the Spirit, himself an agent of diversity, is used by Paul in 12:7 to represent a triune God who is diverse by nature (vv. 4–6). God, as Spirit (v. 4), Lord (v. 5; as v. 3 shows, Paul is thinking of *Lord* as Christ), and God (v. 6), is the common source for spiritual gifts. It can be no accident that Paul begins a section about the variety of spiritual gifts by speaking of the various persons in the Godhead. Moreover, Paul's references to Spirit, Christ, and God later in this section indicate that his tripartite description of God in 12:4–6 is not simply a rhetorical flourish. Although we must not read later trinitarian formulations into Paul's writings, it is hard to avoid the conclusion that Paul sees in the Godhead three distinct persons with full deity.

What does it mean to follow a God like this? Paul is saying, I think, that not only does God affirm diversity in community, but God also models it. John De Gruchy's statement about the Trinity goes to the heart of the matter: "The triune God is not a homogeneous collectivity in which the uniqueness of each person is subsumed within the whole, but a community within which the distinctness of each person is affirmed and therefore within which the other remains a significant other."[14] Diversity, the concept of the "significant other," is built into the system. We must keep in mind, of course, that Paul is speaking about diversity as it occurs within relationships, within community. Although Paul does not define relationships between persons in the Trinity and use them as a starting point (as current theologians might), his central purpose in this section is to show how love governs the use of diverse spiritual gifts. Love recognizes the value of unique gifts and does not try to eliminate them. Love also recognizes that the various gifts must be used in a way that builds up the community. With the spiritual gifts comes a responsibility both to use our gifts for others and to ascertain how other's gifts might benefit us. Following a God who encourages and models diversity means, very simply, that diversity is not something we should fear. Diversity makes a place for the other and values each one's contribution to the community.

It is important to affirm that openness to diverse spiritual gifts means far more than a grudging acknowledgment that "that's the way God wants it" or a half-hearted attempt to avoid squelching someone else's contribution. Diversity is not a burden, but a joy. Diverse spiritual gifts do more than make a community minimally operative; they are God's way of allowing us to experience beauty and richness in our life together. In the last year of his life Dietrich Bonhoeffer spoke several times of the concept of "polyphony," a wonderfully helpful image.[15] While the word *symphony* emphasizes how various sounds work together and is not an inappropriate way of describing the community as body, *polyphony* lays its stress on the value of the diverse sounds. Various harmonies do not detract from the melody or from the unified impact of a piece; rather, they produce a richness and beauty that is far more than just the sum of the parts. Bonhoeffer nowhere applies this image to spiritual gifts, but he does employ it as an affirmation of diverse experiences in the Christian life. Most notable is the way he sees human affection as a counterpoint or alternate melody to God's love, the *cantus firmus*. Both human affection and God's love function in polyphony. They are "undivided and yet distinct," as Chalcedon put it, "like Christ in his divine and human natures." Together they make "a full and perfect sound."[16]

A community that is fed by the incredibly diverse gifts God offers is like beautiful music. Spiritual gifts are polyphonic; their individual sounds do not compete, even if they are unique. The various sounds have a common source in the essential melody, the message of love that God reveals in Jesus Christ; they have a common purpose in believers' love for one another. On the basis of this *cantus firmus* the gifts of the Spirit are free to express wildly different sounds that do not grate on the ear, but produce a rich and full composition. We need to remind ourselves who it is that stands behind these gifts. It is the God of creation, the author of a world of unimaginable variety and fecundity, the God who himself is three in one, who empowers *varieties* of gifts, of services, and of activities (12:4–6). The lists of spiritual gifts Paul offers (12:7–11, 28–30) are just samplers that point to God's extravagance. God chooses to express himself in this way (12:11). Even Paul's abbreviated description of a worship experience (14:27–31; abbreviated, at the very least, because it does not mention the Lord's Supper) mentions far more components than one might consider necessary in a worship service.

The polyphony of spiritual gifts is always most fully expressed in worship. Although Paul's first-century musical experience would probably not have allowed him to understand polyphony as it is conceived by Bonhoeffer, Paul's two musical illustrations in this passage are interesting to note: speaking in tongues, without its *cantus firmus* of love, is like a solitary, noisy instrument (13:1), and the clarity of an individual instrument is not a detraction, but a way of enriching the entire community (14:7–11).

Why do Paul's words about diverse spiritual gifts make those of us in mainstream denominations so nervous? The variety is a problem for us just as it is for the Corinthians. We too champion certain gifts and try to ignore others, although our list of the most and least sought-after gifts is the polar opposite of theirs. In the Christian communities I am a part of, gifts of preaching and teaching and administration occupy the spotlight, gifts of service sit in the last pew, and gifts that more explicitly demonstrate the Spirit's power, such as speaking in tongues, are left outside in the cold. Our reasons for being wary of these diverse gifts parallel those of the Corinthians. Often we believe that certain gifts are optional and that we can refuse them on the basis of our preferences or our definition of what the community needs. Our response to the analogy of the body is usually far less than urgent: we think that perhaps we would be more comfortable without a certain arm or ear or eye.

We need to listen carefully to what Paul is telling the Corinthians. The lesson of the body is that every part is necessary if we are to function at even a basic level. A critical mass of giftedness is absent in communities that declare, subtly but clearly, that if you can't preach or teach or lead, you probably haven't been gifted at all. But the rest of Paul's message is even more important because it is expressed so rarely. Diverse spiritual gifts are about more than efficiency; they are also about what God wants and, indeed, who God is. It is incredibly powerful, in ways that go far beyond the issue of spiritual gifts, to be able to say that God welcomes diversity. How would it shape us if we were able to consistently picture God as community? Most of all, we need to be reminded of the extravagance of a diversely gifted community, one, as Paul imagines, where obscure and often silenced gifts are heard. Think of the fullness, the excitement, the polyphony of worship in which each one has something to contribute, in which wildly different ways of building up the community are experienced (14:26–31)! For many of us in traditions that have too often prized order over varied spiritual gifts, the lure is strong. How can we help the church to see diverse spiritual gifts as something it wants rather than something it only needs?

This question lies at the heart of the more difficult issue: we are wary not just of diverse spiritual gifts, but of any kind of empowerment through the Spirit. One reason for this attitude is confusion about the nature and function of Spirit. Paul helps here, because he affirms that the Spirit is God and that the Spirit has the best interest of the community in mind. The Spirit is not some lesser, ghostlike form of God who makes people do strange things. If we can trust God, we can trust the Holy Spirit. But the more essential reason for our nervousness about the Holy Spirit, I think, has to do with the meaning of the Spirit's empowerment. We rightly sense that it is a sign of the new age. The Corinthians understood this, but they overestimated the extent to which God's kingdom is already here. We, on the other hand, underestimate the kingdom's presence, or at least try to downplay it. If the activity of the Holy Spirit is an indication that God's future has begun to enter our world, then those of us who are eschatologically challenged want nothing to do with it. For those of us who are comfortable with this age and whose only contact with a theology of the end times is with news releases about odd people who predict the exact hour of Christ's return, the Holy Spirit's activity may be something we need, but something we surely do not want. Paul's understanding of communal love, to which we turn next, is one way of addressing this strange dilemma in the contemporary church.

Double Vision

Coming to terms with the community context of chapter 13, as opposed to its typical function in the marriage ceremony, does not necessarily make it easier to apply. After all, it is less difficult to imagine how a young bride and groom might love each other with patience, kindness, endurance, and so on, than to conceive of ourselves loving some of the more crotchety and stubborn members of our congregations in the same way. This tension between what might be called easy love and difficult love is one of the key issues we face as we try to practice love in community. Why is it that the act of loving members of our community can be at times a burden and at other times a joy?

When Paul describes love in 13:4–7, he emphasizes sacrificial action. One can get the feeling that love is about either curtailing personal desires (love is not envious, boastful, or arrogant) or about putting up with those who don't really deserve it (love is patient and kind; it bears all things and endures all things). Love becomes a way of battling a world still filled with sin; it is something we do for others *in spite* of who they are and *in spite* our feelings about them. Time and time again I have heard Christians speak about their love for community members as a burden that has nothing to do with joy-filled relationships; "I will love them," people often say, "but that doesn't mean I have to like them." Jesus' death on the cross can serve as a model for love as sacrificial action. Paul tells the Philippians to give of themselves as Christ gave of himself on the cross (2:3, 8). He tells the Romans that "God proves his love for us in that while we still were sinners Christ died for us" (5:8). We are motivated to act in love toward others in the community, unlovable though they may be, because of the unmerited love we have in Jesus Christ.

But 1 Corinthians 13 goes beyond simply advocating sacrificial duty as the basis of love. Notice how verse 3 asserts that even radical acts for the good of another may not constitute love. At least three of the words used to describe love in verses 4–7 depict loving relationships and strong feelings between community members. We do not, indeed cannot, just *act* in ways that are kind; we must *be* kind (v. 4). And what does it mean to love in such a way that love "believes all things" (v. 7)? Surely it is to affirm the value and potential of the person loved, in much the same way God does with us. The same can be said of a love that "hopes all things" (v. 7; cf. v. 13).

Especially important is Paul's statement that we have been "fully known" by God (v. 12). This is the apostle's shorthand, I think, for describing God's new relationship with us in Jesus Christ (see 8:3). God's future has entered our world. Even though we continue in sin, and even though we still see "dimly" and know "only in part" (v. 12), Paul declares that God sees us as people who "walk in newness of life" (Romans 6:4), who are a "new creation" (2 Corinthians 5:17). God's perception of us as new creatures is the basis for a joyful way of thinking about Christian love. We love others because we can begin to see them as God sees them. Christian love generates its own kind of imagination, as Caroline Simon puts it, one that gives us "a capacity to see people in light of the hope of the wholeness that God intends for them."[17] We love not in spite of what others are, but because they have a real, God-given value and because we need and enjoy them. We are fellow heirs, brothers and sisters in Jesus Christ (Galatians 3:29–4:7). As Paul puts it in 12:26, when "one member suffers, all suffer together with it"; when "one member is honored, all rejoice together with it."

As long as we are still residents of this age, it is probably inevitable that we will experience love both as burden and as joy. The Christian life will be characterized by a type of "double vision," a term Miroslav Volf uses to describe a way of seeing others that is both "from here" and "from there," both from our own limited point of view and from God's.[18] There will always be some in our communities who appear odd to us, people who rub us the wrong way, who have strange ideas and, from our point of view, strange ways of expressing their faith. Loving these people may indeed seem like a burden, consisting of nothing more than steeled interactions that have little hope of blossoming into joyful relationships. But what if we attempt to look at these people not merely as the objects of sacrificial love, but as people whom God considers new creations, people whom God already fully knows? What would it be like to see others as God sees them?

Surely God does not have double vision; both Christ's sacrifice on the cross and God's vision of us as new people are grounded in the same love, a love that seeks a relationship with us. Christ died for us while we were yet sinners, and that act also enables us to be reconciled to God (Romans 5:10). To be justified, according to Paul, is not just to be acquitted by God, but also to enter into a new relationship with him (see especially Romans 3:21–26). Love is not just a way of acting, although it does and must include sacrificial actions toward others. Love is a way of seeing from God's point of view, a desire for fellowship with others, who, like us, have already been declared new creatures. The Christian life can be seen as a process, never fully completed in this age, of allowing God to correct our vision problems. As we are more and more shaped by the joy-filled hope that we know in God, we are thus more able to see others through these same lenses.

The love described in chapter 13 is not only Paul's response to the issue of spiritual gifts, but it is the foundational answer to all the community problems discussed in this letter. God loves us and enables us to love others. Love, with its relationships that believe and hope all things (13:7), is the essence of community. Love is also our surest link with the new age. We experience it now, along with faith and hope and the spiritual gifts, but only love extends into the eschatological future. This understanding of love—as that which defines our future life in God's presence—is the best way of responding to our uneasiness about spiritual gifts and about Christ's new age in general.

Too often we have allowed narrow sectarian views of eschatology to define the passing of this age and the nature of the next. How could we be anything but wary of an eschatology characterized by predictions of the exact date Christ will return, flight from a corrupted world, and wild expressions of spiritual empowerment in worship that are anything but orderly? But the good news is that we need not fear either Christ's second coming or signs of it in the work of the Spirit, because we are already experiencing the love that lies at its heart. We have been allowed to glimpse God's future. We have seen it in God's love for us in Jesus Christ; we have seen it in the life of the community. The spiritual gifts are not "weird magic" best left to those in "other" denominations, as they are too often viewed by those of us in mainline churches. They are simply God's way of empowering us to love one another and to build up the church, especially as we gather to worship. These gifts will be left behind, but the love they represent will remain. God's love is the comforting continuity between this age and the next, that which cannot be removed from us (Romans 8:38–39). It is the essence of the consummated new age Paul longs for (Romans 8:18–19), the time when the double vision of this age will be corrected and we will see God "face to face" (13:12).

Decently and in Order

An amazing transformation comes over the congregation. People who have been dreaming about vacation or worrying about work suddenly become focused. The drowsy wake up, at least for a while. Teenagers stop their flirting and actually listen. The very youngest members of the worshiping community sit in rapt attention. And what is the cause of this congregational fixation, brief though it is? You guessed it: the children's sermon.

When I ask people why they are more attentive during the children's sermon than any other part of worship, I typically receive one of two responses: the preacher is finally speaking at their level, or the young children themselves make for an interesting show. Both of these answers have some merit. But let me suggest another. People listen to children's sermons because they sense that something worshipfully significant might actually happen. In contrast to the rest of the service, highly predictable and scripted, the children's sermon can contain something spontaneous that speaks to the congregation's deepest spiritual needs. Perhaps a three-year-old will ask a question that demands a gut-level response from the pastor. Or perhaps the pastor's words will elicit a spiritually profound statement by a young person that stands on its own and catches people by surprise. Sometimes one of the children will say something that intimates a great spiritual need in her or his family. In the midst of the banter, the shoving, and the silliness, there is always the possibility that God's word might come through the dialogue of the children's sermon in a way that distinguishes that sermon from the rest of the service. The children's sermon commands our attention because we know it is one time in the service when the spiritual gifts of the people, apart from the pastor, might actually be used, in this case the gifts of the youngest members of the community.

What would a contextual theologian like Paul say about spiritual gifts to those of us in mainstream denominations whose problem is ignoring rather than abusing gifts, who have heard "decently and in order" (14:40) and nothing else? He would remind us, I think, that the gifts of the Holy Spirit are not some alien, mysterious force, but simply another way of experiencing God, the same God who comes to us in Jesus Christ. He would tell us that the spiritual gifts are not something to be feared, but are God's way of enabling us to love one another more fully. Even speaking in tongues, when the message is interpreted for all, is desirable. The gifts build up community. Perhaps most of all Paul would remind us that order must not become an obsession. Worship that is Spirit-led is rich and varied; it seeks to use the congregation's diverse gifts.

Imagine what a service based upon 14:26–33 would look like. Each person comes with something to share. There are hymns, teachings, revelations, tongues with interpretations, sermons or prophecies, and even evaluations of these prophecies (v. 29). There are no restrictions other than that the gifts must be intelligible and offered one at a time. Worship would probably assume the form of a crescendoing dialogue in which one gift responds to another. Certainly it would be an intense experience of fellowship, a time when members of the community not only tell of their love for God and one another but also share their deepest spiritual needs.

The difference between this form of worship and what most of us experience on Sunday morning does not mean the Spirit is absent when we meet. Surely the Holy Spirit works in sermons that are painstakingly exegeted and written out in full, and in prayers that are carefully prepared. But we do need to ask ourselves at what point our desire to control worship—indeed, to control all ecclesiastical activity—becomes an attempt to control and even to exclude the Holy Spirit.

In his book with the delightful title *Sacred Cows Make Gourmet Burgers*, William Easum reminds us that doing what we consider the work of the church may not be ministry.[19] Much of what we do—serving on committees, working as an officer of the church, even contributing to worship—can be seen simply as maintenance of an orderly and traditional institution; it might have little to do with our call to love God and those in our community. Even worse, by defining ministry narrowly and by controlling who does what in the church, we could be stifling important spiritual gifts in the congregation. Although Easum perhaps goes too far at times in his criticism of church order, his warning is one we need to hear. Paul insists on the orderly use of gifts during worship, but he never excludes gifts. Implicit in all he says is the trustworthiness of Holy Spirit; the spiritual gifts we receive are valuable and necessary for the life of the community. Those of us who insist that all things in the church be done "decently and in order" need to be reminded that order is defined by the Spirit's control of us, not our control of the Spirit.

Community
and the Resurrection

1 Corinthians 15–16

Does what we believe about life after death affect our understanding of Christian community? Paul would give a resounding "yes" to this question, but I'm not so sure that most mainstream American Christians would answer in the same way. Our conceptions of death and new life can be very foggy. Or if we do have particular views, they often reflect those of society at large and are focused on the experience of the individual. Death is perceived as a solitary passage to a new life that is itself defined by personal views of what constitutes paradise: leisure, hobbies, or whatever else makes life into something that *really* "can't get any better than this."

Our society's views of life after this life are similar in many ways to those held by people in the first-century Greco-Roman world, including the Christians at Corinth. This is exactly why Paul's words about the resurrection of the body in 1 Corinthians 15 are so relevant for us, not only in terms of how this new life is defined but also in terms of how Christian community is and will be experienced. Two related barriers to community lie at the heart of this section of the letter. The first has to do with at least some of the Corinthians' rejection of a bodily resurrection and the effects of that view on both present and future perceptions of community. The second barrier has to do with theological consensus: what does it mean communally when a group of people in the church reject a teaching that is usually understood to be essential to the faith?

151

1 Corinthians 15

Paul's purpose in chapter 15 is to convince the Corinthians that belief in believers' resurrection is an absolutely essential part of the Christian faith. The chapter has two main arguments: verses 1–34 detail why bodily resurrection is important; verses 35–58 explain the nature of the resurrected body. This section of 1 Corinthians is unique because Paul gives little indication that the Corinthians perceive bodily resurrection to be a community issue. Whether there actually were no felt tensions in Corinth concerning resurrection we cannot tell; Paul may simply have chosen not to detail them as he came to the end of what must have been an exhausting letter to write. But it soon becomes clear that a failure to accept believers' resurrection has serious implications for community, whether the Corinthians comprehend them or not.

As we have seen before, Paul does not begin his argument with a concise statement of the problem. That will not come until verse 12. His strategy is instead to remind these people of what they, along with the rest of the church, believe about Christ's resurrection (vv. 1–11). His initial words serve as both an exhortation and a warning. Paul exhorts the Corinthians to hold on to the gospel that he preached and they received, but there is a sense in which their salvation is not a completed act; they are "being saved" and hence need to beware that their faith is not "in vain" (vv. 1–2; cf. vv. 10, 58). Paul makes it clear from the beginning that to reject the gospel message as he proclaims it, including, as he will soon point out, the teaching about the resurrection of the dead, is to put one's salvation in jeopardy. Using the same technical language he employed in 11:23 ("handed on," "received"; v. 3), Paul passes on the authoritative tradition, here in the form a short creedal statement: "that Christ died for our sins in accordance with the scriptures, and that he was buried, and that he was raised on the third day in accordance with the scriptures" (vv. 3–4).

It is the second part of the creed that concerns Paul. Using the very linear action of the perfect tense (*egēgertai*, v. 4), the creed as literally translated tells us that Christ has been raised, or that Christ continues to be the resurrected one (cf. 1:23, where Paul uses the perfect tense to speak of Christ as the crucified one). This resurrection is "in accordance with the scriptures," a further indication of its importance. As if this creedal statement were not enough, Paul adds to it a list of those who saw the resurrected Christ: Cephas (Peter; cf. 1:12); the Twelve; a group of five hundred believers; James, the brother of Jesus; all the apostles; and even Paul himself (vv. 5–8). Again Paul finds it difficult to speak to the Corinthians about himself without going into a defensive posture

(vv. 9–10). He may be "one untimely born" (v. 8; literally, *ektrōma* refers to a fetus that has been aborted) and "the least of the apostles" (v. 9; Did the Corinthians describe him in this way?), but Christ appeared to him in the last of the resurrection appearances (v. 8), and through God's grace he has been a good steward of his call (v. 10).

The point is that the Corinthians believe what Paul has proclaimed and what Christians have witnessed to from the very first: Christ has been raised from the dead (vv. 4, 11). If this is so, Paul argues, how can some of them be so illogical in their thinking that they deny that believers are raised (vv. 12–19)? To reject believers' resurrection is also to reject Christ's resurrection, presumably (although Paul does not give his rationale) because what is not possible for our human bodies could not be possible for Jesus' body (v. 13, 16). And if Christ has not been raised, then the whole of the Christian faith falls like a house of cards. Preaching is in vain, faith has been in vain, and those who proclaim the resurrection have been telling lies about God (vv. 14–15). If Christ has not been raised, then believers are still in their sins (v. 17), because what God does through Christ in the resurrection is not separable from his redemptive act on the cross. Without Christ's resurrection our loved ones who have died no longer exist (v. 18), and we, without any hope for a future life, are pitiable creatures (v. 19). The "some" who suppose they can accept Christ's resurrection but reject that of believers do not know how absurd their stance is; the two resurrections are inseparably linked and absolutely essential to the faith.

The illogic of those who deny believers' resurrection stands in sharp contrast to the message of hope Paul proclaims: Christ has indeed been raised and has put in motion the events of the end times (vv. 20–28). Here Paul shows how thoroughly eschatological his understanding of the resurrection is. As in Jewish apocalyptic scenarios, he assumes that resurrection is to be a corporate event. Therefore, if Christ has been raised, he is the "first fruits" (v. 20), a sure sign that a larger harvest will soon take place. There is a clear sense that God is directing history toward a salvific end. Christ has been sent to undo what Adam did; where there was death, now there will be resurrection (vv. 21–22; cf. vv. 45–49). The events have been ordered: Christ's resurrection takes place first; then, at Christ's return, or coming (*parousia*), believers will be raised (v. 23). "Then comes the end" (v. 24). After the cosmic forces of evil have been destroyed (rulers, authorities, and powers [v. 24]), and after the last great enemy, death, has been subdued (v. 26), Christ hands over the kingdom to the Father (v. 24), and "all things are subjected to him" (vv. 27–28).

For the Corinthians this eschatological statement is powerful because it shows the seriousness with which God takes both the resurrection of believers and death, the reason the resurrection is necessary. Resurrection is not an addendum, a minor theological oddity that one can accept or reject. Christ came to this world in response to death, an intolerable enemy that mars God's creation. The bodily resurrection of believers is the inevitable corporate result of Christ's rising from the dead and is proof of a final victory over death, indeed victory over all those powers that have corrupted this world.

Paul follows this weighty eschatological argument with two that are more practical. Without condoning the strange and otherwise unknown practice of being baptized on behalf of the dead, Paul uses the practice as proof of the Corinthians' implicit affirmation of bodily resurrection (v. 29). And Christian suffering, Paul asserts, makes no sense without the future life of the resurrected body (vv. 30–32). Why, he says hyperbolically, does he "die every day" (v. 30), and why has he "fought with wild animals at Ephesus" (v. 32) if there is nothing beyond this life? Why not rather "eat and drink" and be merry (v. 32)? These two arguments are extremely interesting because they show how difficult it is for Paul to conceive of an afterlife apart from bodily resurrection. One wonders how convincing Paul sounded to the Corinthians at this point. To baptize on behalf of the dead does indicate a belief in the afterlife, but it does not prove that the afterlife must involve the resurrection of the body. And first-century Greco-Roman philosophers gave various definitions of life after death that might have inspired a life of sacrifice. For Paul, however, it is impossible to imagine that any afterlife other than resurrection of the body could inspire Christian discipleship.

Paul concludes this section with the sort of brief ethical exhortation that is so typical of his eschatological statements (vv. 33–34; cf. v. 58; 1 Thessalonians 5:6–11). The imminence of Christ's return never becomes a reason for escapism in Paul; rather, it motivates believers to persevere in the Christian life in the present. Paul tells the Corinthians not to associate with the wrong people (quoting Menander: "Bad company ruins good morals" [v. 33]),[1] but to be sober and to cease their sinning (v. 34). On the one hand this exhortation is aimed specifically at the sin of rejecting the resurrection. The Corinthians are to avoid those who deny the resurrection of the body and to renounce their shameful (v. 34) attitude toward this pivotal teaching. But Paul certainly also intends this to be a comment on the relationship between living in a body in this life and anticipating a resurrected body in the life to come. Several of the Corinthians' sins or problems result from a devaluation of the physical body. Some at Corinth ignore sexual sins (5:1–13; 6:15–20); others think the body's sexual desires can be denied altogether (7:1–7). Some think that feeding their bodies with food offered to idols is of no consequence (10:14–22); others stuff their bodies in the presence of those who are hungry (11:17–22). Some think their bodily appearance is not a matter of community concern (11:2–16). Coming as it does after a warning not to simply "eat and drink" as if there were no tomorrow (v. 32), Paul's exhortation to be sober and right-minded and to avoid sin is surely made with side-glances toward those whose mistreatment of the body reflects a denial of its resurrection.

Although Paul's argument in verses 1–34 is a rhetorical tour de force, it still does not get at the heart of the problem at Corinth. But his probing in the next section (vv. 35–58) certainly does. It is not enough to convince the Corinthians that the resurrection is important; they need to understand how it is possible and that it is even desirable. Employing the diatribe style he uses so successfully in Romans (see Romans 2 and 6),[2] Paul asks the same pointed questions that continue to bother us: "How are the dead raised?" "With what kind of body do they come" (v. 35)?

Like most first-century Jews, Paul believes that the dead will be raised at the consummation of the new age. Christ's resurrection is the first fruits (v. 20) of a resurrection that will include all believers. The problem Paul is encountering is that the Jewish and now Christian doctrine of the resurrection of the body seems odd, even repulsive, to many of the Gentile Christians at Corinth. Dale Martin has documented the wide variety of beliefs concerning afterlife in the first-century Greco-Roman world.[3] Inscriptions indicate that many people expected no existence at all after this life. Others believed the old and less than appealing traditions about Hades or the underworld, where the dead continued to exist as shadowy figures or as corpses in various states of decomposition. Martin also gives examples of healers raising the dead and the dead appearing to living relatives, stories that are common in the popular literature of Paul's day.[4]

But the most significant strand of belief about existence after death, found in the writings of various philosophers and therefore especially among the educated and higher classes, is based on a body/soul dualism. At death the body decomposes; it is left behind by the soul, a higher or finer substance within human beings that wings its way to join the ether (the air or atmosphere) or the divine "out there." Death represents the soul's liberation from the restrictions and anxieties of the body. This liberation allows the soul to be absorbed into the cosmic divine, to achieve a timeless existence but one that is not marked by personal consciousness. As Martin points out, philosophers of the period often preach that death is not an enemy; either there is nothing after death, which brings "the simple absence of sensation," or there is "the departure of the soul to a better place and the return of the body to the earth, of which it was composed."[5]

It is not difficult to imagine how Paul's teaching about the resurrection is received by the primarily gentile audience in Corinth. The phrase
he uses repeatedly throughout chapter 15, "resurrection of the dead"
(*nekros*), would have been interpreted by the Corinthians to mean "resus-
citation of corpses." Many would have been reminded of the ghoulish
existence of those in the underworld or the frightening examples of the
"walking dead" in popular myth or folklore.[6] Others, especially the more
educated, would have considered it ridiculous to speak of the resurrection of a body they knew rotted away after death, a body that must be
left behind so the soul could experience immortality. There was a
tremendous gap in the first century between the Jewish belief in the resurrection of the body (although certainly not all Jews accepted this doctrine) and common gentile beliefs about the fate of the body after death.
Paul may have underestimated this gap and therefore de-emphasized
instruction about the nature of the resurrection on his initial missionary visits. Apparently the Thessalonians first hear about the resurrection of the dead in later correspondence (1 Thessalonians 4:13–5:11).
One wonders if the "some" (v. 12) at Corinth who deny believers' resurrection would have done so if they had been more fully instructed
about the doctrine when Paul was with them.

Because Paul's argument in verses 35–58 is especially about the fea-
sibility of bodily resurrection, it may be, as Dale Martin suggests, that
the "some" Paul is addressing are educated, upper-class Corinthians
who would have been taught to reject any such thinking outright.[7] This
is an interesting theory, and it is consistent with the class conflict we
have seen addressed elsewhere in the letter. Still, it remains speculative,
not only because the chapter lacks explicit references to class tensions,
but also because Paul's words in verses 35–58 and the rest of the chapter address a whole range of Greco-Roman opinions about the resurrection of the body, including those of the lower classes who may think
that resurrection is possible but not necessarily desirable. What is clear
in all of this is Paul's understanding that only *some* reject the resurrection of believers. This means that others do not. Although Paul gives no
indication of tensions this issue might be creating, it is obvious that
there is no agreement in the Corinthian church about the nature of life
after death.

Addressing the straw man as a "fool" may be part of the style of the
diatribe (v. 36; cf. Psalm 14:1), but it also expresses Paul's attitude toward
those whose narrow definition of *body* makes it impossible for them to
accept that people can be raised from the dead. His strategy in verses
35–58 is to get the Corinthians to rethink what *body* might mean, to consider that the new body might be something other than "flesh and blood"
(v. 50). The "some" at Corinth need to comprehend that it really is bod-

ies that are raised; there is continuity between this life and the next. Just as important, they need to understand that these bodies are fit by God for the new age in all its fullness; hence, there is also radical transformation modeled and made possible by the resurrected Christ.

One can answer the fool by pointing to something as simple as a seed and the plant it produces (vv. 36–38). Just as we could never have anticipated what kind of plant a seed might generate, so we cannot presume to know what our new bodies will be like. God designs them according to his creative will (v. 38). But the analogy also suggests continuity between seed and plant, between the former body and the latter body. A seed does not produce just any kind of plant, but one that is consistent with the life it contains. As Paul puts it, God gives "to each kind of seed its own body" (v. 38).

This phrase also implies an endless variety of bodies, and Paul proceeds to illustrate this diversity for the Corinthians. There is more than one kind of flesh in the animal world (v. 39), and there are both heavenly and earthly bodies (v. 40). There is even a hierarchy of bodies that distinguishes between the glory of earthly and heavenly bodies (v. 40), and that within the celestial realm distinguishes the glory of the sun from that of the moon and various stars (v. 41). The Corinthians' rigid definition of the resurrected body is not consistent with the plurality of substances and bodies observable in their own world.

Paul makes the meaning of his analogies explicit in the next paragraph: "So it is with the resurrection of the dead" (v. 42). He uses a series of word pairs to compare the body before and after it has been raised, being careful to use the word *sown* in each case to remind the Corinthians of the continuity and discontinuity between seed and plant. The body is sown perishable, but is raised imperishable; it is sown in dishonor, but is raised in glory; it is sown in weakness, but is raised in power; it is sown a mortal body ("physical" in the NRSV), but is raised a spiritual body (vv. 42–44). What rises is radically transformed, but it is still a body.

Paul's strategy to convince those who object to believers' resurrection, then, is twofold. He is attempting to show them, through his expansive definition of *body,* that resurrection of the body is possible. This is especially important for those whose assumptions about body/soul dualism have made it impossible for them to imagine a body existing in the afterlife. Just as significant, I think, is Paul's attempt to convince the Corinthians that the resurrected body is desirable. The new body will be imperishable (v. 42; cf. 52–54). The word *imperishable* is equated with immortality in verse 54, so it is obviously an appealing way to speak to these Gentile Christians about the new body. The new body will be raised in *glory* (v. 43), a term Paul has used in his description of the eschatological wisdom of believers and the reign of Christ (2:7–8; cf. Philippians 3:21). It will be raised in *power* (v. 43), a word Paul has employed to describe God and his wisdom (1:18, 24; 2:4–5). Perhaps most attractive of all, especially given what we have seen in chapters 12–14, is Paul's description of the resurrected body as a *spiritual* body (v. 44). Think of the appeal this list would have to those at Corinth who believe that a body can exist after death but can imagine it only in terms of ghoulish Greco-Roman myths. Life in the new age will still be in the body, with all the good things that that implies, but the body will be transformed as well, imperishable, filled with God's power and glory, truly spiritual.

Paul's logic and conclusions are powerful, but he knows that if the term *spiritual body* is to be anything other than an oxymoron for the Corinthians it must have a christological foundation. His contrast between mortal body (*psychikos*) and spiritual body (*pneumatikos*, v. 44) grows out of a christological interpretation of Genesis 2:7. Adam, the first man, was a mortal or living being (*eis phychēn zōsaneis*, v. 45, consistent with the Septuagint of Genesis 2:7; the NRSV's translation of *psychikos* as "physical" in vv. 44 and 46 implies, inaccurately, that we are dealing with a distinction between matter and nonmatter). He was dust, bound to this earth in all its corruptibility and transience (v. 47). Christ, the last Adam (v. 45), or second man, is from heaven (v. 47); he has become a life-giving spirit (v. 45). These are the two types of human bodies, and they determine the nature of our bodies in this life and the next. Now we are bodies of dust, bearing Adam's image (vv. 48–49); in the new age we will be spiritual bodies (v. 44), bearing the image of the man of heaven (v. 49). Not only does Christ's resurrected body model what our new bodies will be like but his resurrection also makes such a transformation possible. He is the "life-giving spirit" (v. 45), the "first fruits" (v. 20), the one who makes those who are "in Christ" alive (v. 22).

As we saw in verses 20–28, it is difficult for Paul to speak about the resurrection of the body without also indicating that it is an eschatological issue. One hears this already in the phrase "the last Adam" (v. 45). It is even more obvious in the mini-timeline found in verse 46: "But it is not the spiritual that is first, but the mortal, and then the spiritual." Once again Paul communicates his belief that the movement from mortal to spiritual is part of God's plan. But why does he begin by protesting that the spiritual is not first? Were some at Corinth saying or implying that very thing? Did the "some" to whom Paul refers in verse 12 believe they were already so spiritual that any future spiritual state had little appeal? Verse 46 is the one place in chapter 15 where Paul suggests that the problem he is dealing with is not simply a typical Greco-Roman dislike of resurrected bodies but also a spiritual haughtiness that leads to eschatological confusion.

Paul's affirmation that neither flesh and blood nor what is perishable can inherit the kingdom of God (v. 50), his conclusion to the above argument, sounds very much like the Corinthians' point of view. But there is an essential difference: Paul is talking about new bodies made in the image of the resurrected Christ. The fact that only these new bodies can enter the kingdom raises another important eschatological issue: What happens to those who are still alive when Christ returns (see 1 Thessalonians 4:17)? Paul calls his answer a "mystery" (v. 51), a secret now being revealed through Christ (cf. 2:7), one that he may be telling the Corinthians for the first time. The bombshell is that those who are alive at the *parousia* (the *we* in vv. 51–52 indicates that Paul puts himself in this category, as he does in 1 Thessalonians 4:17) will also be transformed into imperishable, immortal bodies (vv. 52–54). When the trumpet sounds (v. 52, a common apocalyptic image; see Matthew 24:31; Revelation 8–9) and Christ returns, the bodies of all those who are in Christ, both the dead and those who have not experienced death, will "put on immortality" (vv. 53–54).

Once again, Paul's vision for the new body includes both continuity and transformation. The mortal body is transformed into an immortal one (v. 54), but it is still a body. Paul further emphasizes this continuity when he says that our body *puts on* its new imperishability and immortality (vv. 53–54; cf. 2 Corinthians 5:1–10). And as he does in his discussion of the end times in verses 20–28, Paul pictures death, in verses 54–56, as the most significant enemy to be conquered (cf. v. 26). Here the vision of victory over death is even more powerful because of Paul's use of two Old Testament passages. Christ's resurrection and therefore our bodily transformation fulfill Isaiah's longing that death itself will be destroyed (v. 54; Isaiah 25:8). In a free allusion to Hosea 13:14, Paul taunts death as a once powerful but now doomed enemy (v. 55). And ever the theologian, Paul reminds the Corinthians that not just death is conquered through Christ, but also sin, its cause, and the law that empowers sin (v. 56). In Christ is the victory (v. 57) over the most essential enemies we face: sin that alienates us from God, and death, its consequence.

Paul's final word in this section is an exhortation not to sin, or to more accurately convey Paul's mood, an exhortation to continue doing the work of the Lord in this life (v. 58). As was so with verse 34, it is vital that we not see this verse simply as an afterthought. It represents an affirmation or encouragement that the Corinthians recognize that their labor for Christ has not been in vain (cf. v. 2). Even more, it reminds them again that life in this world, in this body, is not unrelated to life in the new age. As we said above, the numerous ways the Corinthians ignore or sin against the body is an indication of how they value it. If the afterlife is a bodiless spiritual existence, if the body is left behind, then perhaps sins against the body are not so important. But Christ's resurrection, along with the incarnation that brought him to our world, is the ultimate affirmation of the physical body. Over and over again in this chapter, Paul has said that for believers life in the new age will be embodied; transformed and spiritual, to be sure, but in the body nevertheless. Christ's resurrection and the promise of new life as spiritual bodies should motivate the Corinthians to take their current life as embodied disciples very seriously.

In communal terms, the Corinthians' rejection of a future bodily existence is also a temptation to ignore the bodies of their fellow Christians and hence the church as the body of Christ. If neither bodies nor personal identity continue after death, what motivation is there to love other embodied beings in the present? Without these new bodies that guarantee a continuity of love, precisely as Paul describes in 13:8–13, it becomes all too easy to assume that community, like embodied existence, will be left behind at death. But, Paul explains, the new age in Christ is anything but a solitary, disembodied life. Christ's resurrection is the first fruits of a corporate resurrection (v. 23). When the trumpet sounds and Christ returns, the whole community, both the dead and the living (v. 51–52), will together be transformed into new spiritual bodies. People will be raised as beings who are conscious of their former lives but no longer fear death (vv. 54–56), who bask in communal and divine love (13:8–13), and submit to God's lordship (v. 28). First Corinthians 15 is Paul's reminder to the Corinthians that their life together after Christ's return must serve as the vision that defines and empowers community in the present.

1 Corinthians 16

Chapter 16 contains Paul's typical final messages and greetings, a major shift from the content of the previous chapter. Nevertheless, issues relating to Christian community continue to prevail here in the final words of what must have been an extremely taxing letter to write. Of primary importance is the way Paul links the Corinthians with the wider Christian community. They are reminded that Paul intends to receive a collection soon for the church at Jerusalem; he will send the collection to Jerusalem through the Corinthians' own couriers (vv. 1–4; cf. 2 Corinthians 8–9). Paul mentions other churches and mission fields (vv. 8–9, 19) as well as other widely scattered Christians the Corinthians know (vv. 10, 12, 19–20). Community clearly extends beyond the house churches of Corinth.

As a good pastor who is aware of the Corinthians' communal history, Paul also anticipates tensions and discreetly deals with them. Paul encourages them to treat Timothy with respect (vv. 10–11); he knows this letter may be volatile and that Timothy will bear the brunt of the criticism. Paul assumes there will be disappointment because Apollos will not be visiting, and he offers some explanation (v. 12). In the case of Stephanas, Fortunatus, and Achaicus (vv. 15–18), the apostle is determined that these men who have been his supporters (see 1:16) and who will probably bear this letter to the church must not be the cause of further division. Paul urges the Corinthians to recognize them and work with them, not because of their relationship to him, but because these men have shown what it means to give themselves in service to others (v. 15). We see Paul putting out communal fires to the very end of the letter.

The same awareness of the needs of the Corinthian community is found in Paul's final exhortations and blessings. His encouragement to "keep alert, stand firm in your faith, be courageous, be strong" (v. 13), indicating the need to live distinctive Christian lives because of the imminence of the new age, is highly relevant in light of the Corinthians' eschatological confusion. Similarly, his invitation to the Lord to return (v. 22; "Our Lord, come"; *maranatha*) reminds the Corinthians that the new age has not yet arrived in its fullness. Note especially Paul's focus on love, the key to community that he emphasizes throughout the letter. Everything the Corinthians do must be done in love (v. 14). Those who have no love for Christ stand accursed (*anathema*, v. 22); the community has ethical and theological boundaries that have their foundation in love. They are to greet one another with the holy kiss (v. 20), to perform a very embodied act of love that, considering the divisions at Corinth, may have been extremely difficult for them to do. And after the traditional benediction of grace (v. 23), the apostle closes with a blessing of love (v. 24), telling the Corinthians that his love, the love they share in Jesus Christ, will continue to be with them.

Hopefully the Corinthians are able to hear Paul's message. We know from 2 Corinthians that before the situation is resolved it will worsen, especially in terms of the church's relationship to Paul. But the fact that this correspondence has been preserved indicates that at least some of the Corinthians believe Paul's words to be valuable. Paul's final words are a powerful testimony to the love that has transformed him and made him into the pastor and missionary that he is, the same love he hopes will dissolve the tensions at Corinth. The final blessing in verse 24 is very similar in content to 11:1: "Be imitators of me, as I am of Christ." Throughout the letter Paul has held up Christ as the model for the love that can bind a community together. And Paul boldly tells the Corinthians to imitate him as well, because he believes that he is a powerful example of what happens when one is engulfed by this love. Surely this letter supports that confidence. In spite of the anger and sorrow Paul expresses toward this congregation, he continues to love them in ways that might surprise those who do not understand his love's origin. He is both pastor and protective parent (4:14) to the very end of the letter. Paul believes that the love he has received and now models will heal this troubled community.

Paul's Words for the Contemporary Community

Putting on the Imperishable Body

Our fear of death in American society has made dying into an incredibly private affair, but even more problematic is the way we as contemporary American Christians envision our passage to and experience of the afterlife. In scores of sermons and in the words of countless individuals, I have heard our entrance into heaven described as a solitary journey. Aunt So and So "has gone to heaven," or "has gone to meet her maker," we like to say, meaning that she is bound for heaven as an individual soul. Our jokes about the departed standing alone before St. Peter, taking some sort of admissions test, reflect what many Christians believe. It is amazing how similar stories of this solitary quest for heaven are to those found in Greco-Roman literature, whether tales of the lonely journey to Hades or of the soul's obstacle-filled flight back to the cosmic divine. When entrance into heaven is defined primarily as something that happens to the individual soul at death, it is difficult to conceive of it as having much to do with community.

Anecdotal evidence also suggests that most Christians in mainline denominations don't concern themselves very much with the nature of the future life. I am surprised at how many people, when asked to define the afterlife, follow their cursory statements about living in the presence of God with definitions that usually reflect little more than each individual's assessment of what is good and pleasurable in this life. Life in heaven will include one's favorite hobbies of golf or gardening, and ongoing relationships with family members. It is inevitable, I suppose, that people define the afterlife in terms of what they know and love in this life, especially when most churches offer only minimal instruction on the subject. On the positive side, these common depictions of heaven do convey a belief in the ongoing consciousness of the individual Christian, a belief with which Paul would agree. Problematic, however, is the lack of concern for Christian community, at least apart from biological family. How is it possible that we who claim to be defined by love can have so little desire for and knowledge of an afterlife filled to overflowing with relationships with fellow believers?

Our views of the afterlife are the product of a church that has too often ignored traditional eschatology, that is, an awareness of Christ's second coming and the resurrection of the body that will occur at that time. Like the Corinthians, we desperately need to hear Paul's depiction of the new life in Christ. I have often wondered if we would be more attentive students of Paul if he had been a visual artist rather than a writer. We live in a highly visual society, and especially as Protestants we are starved for ways we might appropriate the gospel that go beyond the auditory. Paul, of course, was not a painter (at least we have no evidence that he was), but we do possess many visual interpretations of the *parousia* that beg to be compared with what the apostle says in chapter 15.

Two paintings by Stanley Spencer (1891–1959) are especially interesting because they portray not the typical apocalyptic themes of God's wrath and cataclysmic destruction, but people who are in the process of rising from the dead. In his painting called *The Resurrection, Cookham* (1924–25) Spencer shows graves being opened in the cemetery at his home church in Cookham, England. In a scene filled with sunshine and flowers, individuals emerge from their plots and families from their crypts. Some are naked, while others are still dressed in their grave clothes. Near a sunny church wall are Christ, Moses, and other prominent figures. The scene looks like the rousing hour at a giant slumber party; the recently revived are looking about, sleepy-eyed, contemplating what this mass opening of the graves is all about. Those who have been raised are beginning to recognize one another, to touch and chat.

In another painting, *The Resurrection of the Soldiers* (1927–32), Spencer deals with the resurrection in a similar way, although the setting is a World War One battlefield and cemetery. Soldiers are rising, and they too look both dazed from their long sleep and amazed by this return to life. Some, apparently not knowing what to do with themselves, have returned to tasks that had been interrupted by death: rolling bandages and barbed wire or cleaning their uniforms. Others greet their fellow soldiers, perhaps former enemies, with handshakes. The crosses that marked their graves are being pushed aside and piled up, and some of the men are bringing the crosses to Christ, a rather minor figure in the rear of the scene. Even the mules lost in battle are coming back to life.[8]

The impact of Spencer's paintings is undeniable: what a strange and wonderful teaching that of the resurrection of the dead is. It is impossible to avoid experiencing the same awe we see in the faces of the newly raised in these paintings. Bodies will actually be raised from the dead! Creation itself will participate in this renewal! However, Spencer's paintings, creative interpretations of this amazing event, do stand in tension with 1 Corinthians 15. There is little sense, for instance, that the new age will be a joyful celebration of God's mercy and love, although this theme is implicit everywhere in Paul's words. Also, Spencer appears to be portraying a general resurrection, whereas Paul's focus is on the resurrection of believers. He does not present a clear depiction of life in *spiritual* bodies, although it must be admitted that the nature of such bodies might be difficult to communicate visually. What I like best about these paintings, though, is the way they confront us with the communal nature of entrance into the consummated new age. As when we read Paul, we get no sense that this is a solitary journey. When Christ returns, all believers who have died will together rise to new life (15:23, 52). Even more, according to Paul, those who are alive will be transformed (vv. 52–53) and will join the crowd. Spencer's paintings allow us to see what we only hear in Paul, that from the beginning we will experience this new life in the presence of others who have been raised by God.

This does not mean that we must avoid comforting ourselves with the belief that our departed loved ones have gone to be with God. Paul himself uses this sort of language. In Philippians 1:23 he says he longs to depart from this life so that he can be with Christ, and he tells the Christians at Rome that death cannot separate them from God's love in Christ (Romans 8:38–39). Paul never addresses what we might consider to be chronological tensions between this understanding of the afterlife, on the one hand, and the resurrection that occurs when Christ returns, on the other. Perhaps he is more willing to live with the unknowable than we are, or perhaps he assumes that God's conception of time is not like ours (see 2 Peter 3:8). Two things are clear, however. Paul is so confident of God's care for believers within the movement of salvation history that he believes that nothing, not even death, can remove us from God's loving presence. Even more important for our purposes, the bodily resurrection at the *parousia* is by far Paul's clearest and most essential way of speaking about the new age (see, for instance, later references to the resurrection in Philippians 3:10–11, 20–21). The word *heaven* should bring to mind a community of bodies rising together at Christ's return and living together in his love, not a solitary and bodiless soul finding its way back to God.

In the new age we will be "spiritual bodies" (15:44). Our questions about what this might mean are probably very similar to those the Corinthians asked. Will we have the same molecules or substance as before? Will we have the same ailments? What will we look like? Paul answers these questions, at least in a general sort of way, in his affirmation that our bodies will be transformed, or *spiritual*. We will be imperishable, filled with glory and power (vv. 42–43), and immortal (vv. 53–54), something other than flesh and blood (v. 50). Death, the ultimate fear of those confined to the body, will be conquered. We will bear the image of the resurrected Christ (v. 49) and leave behind all those things that link our bodies with the corruptibility of this age. It is true that this radical transformation of both dead and living bodies remains a mystery in terms of its details, even though Paul calls the transformation of living bodies a mystery revealed (v. 51). But surely we know enough: the weakness and mortality of the body we inherited from Adam will be gone (vv. 47–49).

But then the question becomes, What continuity is there between this body and the body we will be given? If we become immortal and imperishable, in what sense will we still be bodies? The basis of the answer is Paul's assumption that there will be continuity between the old and new body in terms of personal consciousness or identity, as was so for Christ. Paul, like any Jew of his day, could not imagine people apart from the bodies that link them with the drama of salvation in this world. The Greco-Roman doctrine of souls losing themselves in a union with the divine and escaping from the endless cycles of history, is the polar opposite of Paul's thought. God works in this world, wooing us to him in the complexities of time and space.

Like his contemporary Jewish apocalyptic thinkers, Paul finds it impossible to envision a new age that does not include a transformation of the cosmos, a time when "creation itself will be set free from its bondage to decay" (Romans 8:21). Though the world that God declared "very good" (Genesis 1:31) is temporarily "subjected to futility" (Romans 8:20), it is itself worthy of salvation. But for Paul the Christian, the ultimate affirmation of God's continued love for his creation is expressed in the human body: God sent his Son into the world as a body, and as a body he conquered death, the greatest threat to bodily existence (1 Corinthians 15:26, 54–56). God's ongoing concern for us as bodies in the sweep of salvation history is a declaration that our experience as bodies in this world is not unimportant or disposable. Rather, it gives us an identity that marks even our future relationship with God. Put simply, *you* will be raised bodily: you will know who you are, and others will recognize you. God will know us, and we as individuals will know God.

Obviously Paul does not imagine the new age in terms of isolated bodies: it is his assumption that relationships are an inevitable part of the continuity of existence that the body represents. Paul has already told us that the new age is a manifestation of love (13:13). Now, in chapter 15, he completes the picture by naming that love's recipients: those who are raised in Christ (v. 22) will receive the fullness of God's love. And as bodies, as conscious beings, we will continue to express the love we have known in this world. Certainly God, the one to whom all things are to be subjected (vv. 27–28), will be the focus of our love (see 1 Thessalonians 4:17), but firmly imbedded in Paul's corporate understanding of the new age is the belief that love among believers will continue as well. As he demonstrates over and over again in his letters and especially 1 Corinthians 13, love expressed in community is an inevitable outgrowth of love received from God. Of course, it is precisely these new bodies, bodies that have both a personal identity and a capacity to love, that allow us to have relationships with one another. This theme of the new communion among the raised is an essential way of understanding how Adam's legacy of hate and division is undone (vv. 47–49). Paul is saying that the new age will consist of a community of believers in bodily form, of people who are able to give and receive love.

Community is not something we leave behind when Christ returns. The love we now receive in the body of Christ is a foretaste of what we will know as spiritual bodies, when we are united with that great "cloud of witnesses" (Hebrews 12:1), resurrected Christians from every time and place. Paul's use of the phrase *spiritual body* also sets limits on what we can know about this transformed body and how it will function in community. Surely bodies that have left weakness and dishonor behind (15:43) will no longer be subject to the community problems we now live with. But how does the word *spiritual* define the function of the body and therefore the expression of love? Will our bodies have the same senses we now have? Will we relate to one another sensually? Will we be able to enjoy the beauty of the restored creation together (Romans 8:18–25; Colossians 1:20)? Will these new bodies allow us to work together and use our gifts for one another? For us, as I'm sure was so for the Corinthians, Paul raises more questions than he answers.

Paul does, however, give us an incredible picture of the new age, bare-bones though it is. Scott Cairns's poem "Loves: Magdalen's Epistles" is a reminder not to let these unanswered questions diminish the uniqueness and power of Paul's revelation about the centrality of body.[9] The narrator is Mary Magdalene, here defined traditionally as a woman of ill repute who was saved by Jesus (John 8:1–11) and who anointed his feet (Luke 7:36–50). Against so-called loftier conceptions, she proclaims a message that grows out of her own earthy life experience: "all loves are bodily." For those who follow the Christ who took on human form, any division between what some believe is the purity of the spirit and the dishonor of the body is a false dichotomy, the illegitimate presumption of "dissecting *the person* into something less complex."

Like this Mary, Paul sees us as complicated beings, a wonderful mix of personal identity and sensual and spiritual awareness best described as *body*. And as bodies we may bear the mark of corruption that came in Adam, but we are still God's good creation, worth the sacrifice Jesus Christ made in the flesh. Paul's astounding eschatological message in chapter 15 is precisely that "all loves are bodily."

Of course Cairns is using Mary's words to address the intersection of body and love in *this* life, but there is almost always a link between one's understanding of the present body and of the future body. Most probably the same Corinthians who deny believers' resurrection devalued their present bodies as well. How does it affect us as community *now* if we actually believe that God's kingdom will consist of bodies raised to new communion with one another? Certainly we would honor our bodies now (see 6:19), especially in ways that are related to issues of purity in the community (cf. chapters 5–6). But I find it especially fascinating to think about how a vision for a bodily and communal future should affect our present relationships and how we now honor the bodies of others. Can we ignore the suffering and loneliness of bodies that God will raise in the new age, those very bodies that will make up our future community? Can we continue to nurse a lifelong hatred of certain people if we know they will be our sisters and brothers in the new age? Can we continue to foster class distinctions in the church that treat some bodies as less worthy? What does it say about the vitality of our communities if we live unaware of the new age and Christ's return, or at least unaware that life in heaven will be a bodily existence? Paul's words in chapter 15 are incredibly important for the contemporary mainstream church not only because we need to be molded by an eschatological vision but also because the content of Paul's vision, a new body and its impact upon community, is one we so often neglect to teach.

Theological Boundaries

There is another community issue that lies just beneath the surface in chapter 15, one that is here linked with the resurrection of the body, but one that could occur in any situation when a teaching that is essential to the faith is at stake. Paul's words in chapter 15 force us to ask ourselves, "How do theological tensions affect community? At what point does theological error disrupt community to the extent that it becomes a disciplinable issue?" We have seen Paul's quick and bold response to moral maladies, most notably his declaration that the man living with his stepmother must be driven out from the Corinthians' midst (5:13). His action is an attempt to preserve both the purity of the community (5:6–8) and, most probably, its image in the world (5:1, 9–13). Usually the behavioral issues at Corinth indicate a skewed theology: their love for rhetorical wisdom, for example, results from their failure to grasp the meaning of the cross (1:17–2:5). This may be a simple theological misunderstanding, but at other times the error appears to be more dangerous and intentional. The larger ethical issue of the Corinthians' disrespect for the body has its origin in a denial of believers' resurrection, as we have seen. And Paul states unequivocally that a rejection of this resurrection is a rejection of Christ's resurrection, and hence a rejection of the entire gospel message (15:12–19). This is clearly a theological problem that the community cannot overlook.

If some deny the resurrection and others support Paul's position, it is not hard to picture the intense community problems that would be created, even apart from the "body" issues dealt with in this letter. Think of the mistrust! Imagine how difficult it would be to define or engage in corporate mission or even to speak a common faith language! We have no trouble understanding the relationship between theological foundations and community formation in the Corinthian church because the issue has remained essentially unchanged all these years. Indeed, many of us have experienced firsthand the Corinthians' plight in a contemporary church that has too often assumed that our practice of the inclusive love of the gospel requires us to sacrifice our theological standards. Is it possible to have Christian fellowship or to receive the sacrament with those whom you believe have rejected the heart of the gospel?

In the middle of the second century, at a time when rejection of a bodily resurrection was becoming more widespread under the Gnostics and Marcion, Polycarp stated in no uncertain terms, "Whoever denies both resurrection and judgment—such one is the first-born of Satan."[10] It is obvious how he would deal with the "some" (15:12) at Corinth who question whether believers are raised from the dead! Paul is much more equivocal as he writes to his children in the faith (4:14). He begins chapter 15 by suggesting that some may have come to believe "in vain" (v. 14). Yet after clearly identifying the Corinthians' theological error (vv. 12–19) and its shamefulness (v. 34), Paul very intentionally concludes with words of encouragement rather than judgment or exclusion: "Therefore, my beloved, be steadfast, immovable, always excelling in the work of the Lord, because you know that in the Lord your labor is not in vain" (v. 58). This is Paul's typical strategy with these new Christians, as we have seen over and over again. Even in chapters 5 and 6, where he is moved initially by the need to discipline the errant individual and issues a strong warning to the congregation (5:2, 6), he closes with conciliatory reminders of who they are in Jesus Christ: "But you were washed, you were sanctified, you were justified in the name of our

Lord Jesus Christ and in the Spirit of our God" (6:11); "For you were bought with a price; therefore glorify God in your body" (6:20).

Paul's patience with the Corinthians as they wrestle with the tensions between their new faith and their Greco-Roman ideology must not lull us into thinking that he has no theological absolutes. In 12:3 Paul tells his hearers, "I want you to understand that no one speaking by the Spirit of God ever says 'Let Jesus be cursed!'" Even stronger is his pronouncement in the final paragraph of the letter: "Let anyone be accursed who has no love for the Lord" (16:22). It is interesting to note that if he is speaking about members of the Corinthian church in these statements, he does so indirectly rather than by making personal attacks. But Paul obviously is aware of the limits of theological deviation, even though he chooses to use this awareness to motivate these young Christians at Corinth rather than embark on a theological witch-hunt. For the opposite tactic one need only look to Paul's letter to the Galatians, where the outsiders who are endangering the church by proclaiming a law-based message are openly declared anathema (1:6–9). On the basis of Galatians, we might say that theological error becomes "disciplinable" for Paul when it intentionally and openly rejects an essential part of the gospel message and when it does so in a way that threatens the faith of a Christian community.

If Paul sets ethical boundaries, he certainly also sets theological boundaries. It is conceivable, I suppose, that this awareness of theological absolutes might force the use of church discipline in specific cases, just as church discipline can be necessary for ethical violations. But my real motivation in stressing theological boundaries lies in a desire for the church to rediscover its theological heritage. Theologizing is not just an unnecessary "head game," reserved primarily for professionals. There is always a link between how we live and how we think about God and our salvation: sometimes our theology defines our actions; at other times our actions create our theology. Theology is simply what we say or think when we are asked why we act as we do as Christians. It is an unavoidable and necessary part of the Christian life. And Paul forces us to consider again that not every theology is acceptable; our theology must be correct. But how do we measure theological truth? Who or what is the standard for theological integrity? Paul's words are an invitation to swim against the stream of theological lethargy so many of us experience in our churches, to discover who we are and are not theologically, to know the sources for our theological truth, to learn what it means to be Methodist or Reformed or Lutheran or Catholic or Baptist.

In discovering who we are theologically we also discover a common language that binds us together as community. When considering the origin of community problems, we often rightly think of class differences, personal conflict, selfishness, societal pressures, and so on. But we usually underestimate the effects of an absence of theological communication. One of the most joy-filled experiences I can have as a visiting preacher is to enter a church I know nothing about and, through conversation and worship, to quickly discover that we talk the same theological language. We have the same faith, we use the same words to describe it, and we rely on the same biblical and creedal resources. It's an experience akin to discovering a long-lost family, and I never cease to be amazed by its power. Perhaps it is a foretaste of the new age. Christian community is not simply a gathering of people who are nice to each other. It is a gathering of people who love each other because God first loved them, people who know the common source of their love and who have a common language to share its wonder.

Notes

Introduction

1. Robert D. Putnam's analysis of five independent survey archives in *Bowling Alone: The Collapse and Revival of American Community* (New York: Simon and Schuster, 2000), 70–72, 75–79.

2. George Gallup Jr., *The Unchurched American—10 Years Later* (Princeton, N.J.: Princeton Religion Research Center, 1988); see comments by Robert Wuthnow, *Sharing the Journey: Support Groups and America's New Quest for Community* (New York: The Free Press, 1994), 38–39.

3. The church that models community during one's childhood is often very formative. I continue to be shaped by the love of the First Reformed Church, Maurice, Iowa.

4. Putnam, *Bowling Alone*, 283. See this page for a summary of Putnam's interpretation of the decline of civic community.

5. For a helpful description of American individualism, especially as it relates to religious expression, see William A. Dyrness, *How Does America Hear the Gospel?* (Grand Rapids: Eerdmans, 1989), 83–105.

6. For an introduction to postmodernism, see Stanley J. Grenz, *A Primer on Postmodernism* (Grand Rapids: Eerdmans, 1996).

7. Robert Bellah, Richard Madsen, William M. Sullivan, Ann Swidler, and Steven M. Tipton, *Habits of the Heart: Individualism and Commitment in American Life* (Berkeley: University of California Press, 1985), 221.

8. Ibid., 282.

9. Wuthnow, *Sharing the Journey*, 16.

10. Ibid., 35.

11. See Ralph P. Martin, *The Family and the Fellowship: New Testament Images of the Church* (Grand Rapids: Eerdmans, 1979), 34–45, and Robert J. Banks, *Paul's Idea of Community: The Early House Churches in Their Historical Setting* (Grand Rapids: Eerdmans, 1980), 60–61, for helpful discussions of *koinōnia*.

12. Robin Scroggs, *Paul for a New Day* (Philadelphia: Fortress, 1977), 7.

13. See Virginia Wiles, *Making Sense of Paul: A Basic Introduction to Pauline Theology* (Peabody, Mass.: Hendrickson, 2000), 15–17, for a clear discussion of types of eschatology as they relate to Paul.

14. Avery Dulles, *Models of the Church* (New York: Doubleday, 1987).

15. See Jerome Murphy-O'Conner, *Paul, A Critical Life* (Oxford: Oxford University Press, 1997), 252–317, for an excellent overview of historical issues relative to Corinth.

16. Walter Schmithals, *Gnosticism in Corinth: An Investigation of the Letters to the Corinthians* (Nashville: Abingdon, 1971); Hans Conzelmann, *1 Corinthians* (Philadelphia: Fortress, 1975).

17. Gerd Theissen, *The Social Setting of Pauline Christianity: Essays on Corinth* (Philadelphia: Fortress, 1982); Dale Martin, *The Corinthian Body* (New Haven: Yale University Press, 1995).

18. Antoinette Wire, *The Corinthian Women Prophets: A Reconstruction through Paul's Rhetoric* (Minneapolis: Fortress, 1990).

19. Scott Cairns, "The Entrance of Sin," in *Recovered Body* (New York: George Braziller, 1998), 40.

Chapter 1

1. See James L. Bailey and Lyle D. Vander Broek, *Literary Forms in the New Testament: A Handbook* (Louisville: Westminster/John Knox, 1992), 23–30, for an introduction to the Pauline letter form.

2. See Conzelmann, *1 Corinthians* (Philadelphia: Fortress, 1975); Schmithals, *Gnosticism in Corinth: An Investigation of the Letters to the Corinthians* (Nashville: Abingdon, 1971); and Birger Albert Pearson, *The Pneumatikos-Psychikos Terminology of 1 Corinthians* (Missoula: Society of Biblical Literature, 1973).

3. See Duane Litfin, *St. Paul's Theology of Proclamation: First Corinthians 1–4 and Greco-Roman Rhetoric* (Cambridge: Cambridge University Press, 1994); Stephen Pogoloff, *Logos and Sophia: The Rhetorical Situation of 1 Corinthians* (Atlanta: Scholars Press, 1994); Michael A. Bullmore, *St. Paul's Theology of Rhetorical Style: An Examination of 1 Corinthians 2:1–5 in the Light of First-Century Greco-Roman Culture* (San Francisco: International Scholars, 1995).

4. For an extended comment on Favorinus and an excellent overview of Greco-Roman rhetoric see Litfin, *St. Paul's Theology*, 21–146.

5. Annie Dillard, *An American Childhood* (New York: Perennial Library, 1988), 196.

6. Ibid., 194–195.

7. Ibid., 198–199.

Chapter 2

1. In the Greek text it is not at all clear where the prepositional phrase "in the name of the Lord Jesus" should be located. One legitimate option is to make it follow the phrase "the one who has done this thing," thus emphasizing that the man's immorality has a theological rationale (v. 4).

2. See comment by Richard B. Hays, *First Corinthians* (Louisville: John Knox, 1997), 83.

3. Brian S. Rosner, "Temple and Holiness in 1 Corinthians 5," *Tyndale Bulletin* 42, no. 1 (1991):135–145. See Rosner's collection of articles on 1 Corinthians in his *Paul, Scripture, and Ethics: A Study of 1 Corinthians 5–7* (Grand Rapids: Baker, 1999).

4. Brian S. Rosner, "OUXI MALLON EPENΘHSATE: Corporate Responsibility in 1 Corinthians 5," *New Testament Studies* 38 (1992):470–473.

5. Dale Martin, *The Corinthian Body* (New Haven: Yale University Press, 1995), 76–79.

6. *The Age of Innocence*, directed by Martin Scorsese; screenplay by Jay Cocks and Martin Scorsese (Columbia, 1993).

7. "Letter CCXVII, To Amphilochius, on the Canons," in *St. Basil: Letters and Select Works*, *The Nicene and Post-Nicene Fathers*, ed. Philip Schaff and Henry Wace (Grand Rapids: Eerdmans, 1955), 256.

Chapter 3

1. See discussion in Elisabeth Schüssler Fiorenza, *In Memory of Her: A Feminist Theological Reconstruction of Christian Origins* (New York: Crossroad, 1984), 224–225. Except for the aristocracy and cultic females, "virginity was a privilege and not a right according to Roman law."

2. Gordon Fee, in *The First Epistle to the Corinthians* (Grand Rapids: Eerdmans, 1987), 518–521, has a very thorough discussion of the difficulties of this verse.

3. So argues Fiorenza in *In Memory of Her*, 229, following J. Kurzinger, "Frau und Mann nach 1 Kor 11.11f," *Biblische Zeitschrift* 22 (1978): 270–275.

4. See Judith M. Gundry-Volf, "Gender and Creation in 1 Corinthians 11:2–16: A Study of Paul's Theological Method," in *Schriftauslegung-Evangelium-Kirche*, ed. Otfried Hofius et al. (Gottingen: Vandenhoeck and Ruprecht, 1997), 151–171; and Miroslav Volf, *Exclusion and Embrace: A Theological Exploration of Identity, Otherness, and Reconciliation* (Nashville: Abingdon, 1996), 186–187.

5. John Gray, *Men Are from Mars, Women Are from Venus* (New York: HarperCollins, 1992).

6. Mary Field Belenky, Blyth McVicker Clinchy, Nancy Rule Goldberger, and Jill Mattuck Tarule, *Women's Ways of Knowing: The Development of Self, Voice, and Mind* (New York: Basic Books, 1986), 100–130.

7. Deborah Tannen, *You Just Don't Understand: Women and Men in Conversation* (New York: William Morrow and Company, 1990), 74–95.

8. See similar conclusions in Nancy J. Duff's helpful chapter "Vocation, Motherhood, and Marriage," in *Women, Gender, and Christian Community*, ed. Jane Dempsey Douglas and James F. Kay (Louisville: Westminster, 1997), 69–81.

9. A phrase used by Richard B. Hays in his commentary *First Corinthians* (Louisville: John Knox, 1997), 191.

10. Volf, *Exclusion and Embrace*, 184.

11. For an excellent discussion of this issue see Caroline J. Simon, *The Disciplined Heart: Love, Destiny, and Imagination* (Grand Rapids: Eerdmans, 1997), especially the chapter "Friendship between the Sexes."

12. Simon, *Disciplined Heart*, 149.

13. Ibid., 151.

14. Barbara Kingsolver, *The Poisonwood Bible* (New York: Harper Flamingo, 1998), 89.

Chapter 4

1. For background information on meat sacrificed to idols, see W. L. Willis, *Idol Meat in Corinth: The Pauline Argument in 1 Corinthians 8 and 10* (Chico, Calif.: Society of Biblical Literature Dissertation Series, 1985), 17–61; Peter D. Gooch, *Dangerous Food: 1 Corinthians 8–10 in its Context* (Waterloo, Ontario: Wilfrid Laurier University Press, 1993), 53–60.

2. Gerd Theissen, *The Social Setting of Pauline Christianity: Essays on Corinth* (Philadelphia: Fortress, 1982), 121–144.

3. The Shema is the traditional declaration of the oneness and sovereignty of God: "Hear, O Israel: The LORD is our God, the LORD alone" (Deuteronomy 6:4).

4. See Victor Paul Furnish, *The Theology of the First Letter to the Corinthians* (Cambridge: Cambridge University Press, 1999), 70–75.

5. Gordon Fee's argument in *The First Epistle to the Corinthians* (Grand Rapids: Eerdmans, 1987), 357–363, is typical.

6. Would compensation for Paul have created a financial burden for the Corinthians or obligated him in some undesirable way? For a discussion of this question, see 2 Corinthians 11:7–9; 12:13.

7. Jewish legend speaks of a rock following them in the desert: Paul sees this as a type for Christ (v. 4).

8. William A. Dyrness, *How Does America Hear the Gospel?* (Grand Rapids: Eerdmans, 1989), 48–53.

9. Lesslie Newbigin, *Foolishness to the Greeks: The Gospel and Western Culture* (Grand Rapids: Eerdmans, 1986), 20.

10. Martin Luther, "The Freedom of a Christian," in *Luther's Works*, vol. 31, ed. H. J. Grimm (Philadelphia: Muhlenberg, 1957), 344.

11. *Institutes of the Christian Religion*, vols. 21 and 22 in *The Library of Christian Classics*, ed. John T. McNeill, trans. Ford Lewis Battles (Philadelphia: Westminster, 1967), 3.19.7.

12. John Updike, "Short Easter," in *The Afterlife and Other Stories* (New York: Alfred A. Knopf, 1994).

13. Ibid., 102.

14. *The Matrix*, directed and written by Larry Wachowski and Andy Wachowski (Warner Brothers, 1999).

15. Abraham J. Heschel, *The Prophets*, vol. 2 (New York: Harper, 1962), 191.

Chapter 5

1. Robert J. Banks, *Paul's Idea of Community: The Early House Churches in Their Historical Setting* (Grand Rapids: Eerdmans, 1980), 34–37.

2. Gordon Fee, *The First Epistle to the Corinthians* (Grand Rapids: Eerdmans, 1987), 537.

3. Jerome Murphy-O'Conner, *St. Paul's Corinth: Tests and Archaeology* (Wilmington, Del.: Michael Glazier, 1983), 153–161.; cf. Gerd Theissen, *The Social Setting of Pauline Christianity: Essays on Corinth* (Philadelphia: Fortress, 1982), 145–174.

4. Richard L. Rohrbaugh, "The Social Location of the Markan Audience," *Interpretation* 47 (1993): 382–387.

5. See Theissen, *Social Setting*, 94–95, for a more complete list.

6. Ibid., 75–83.

7. Ibid., 102 (emphasis mine).

8. For descriptions of postmodernism see Frederic B. Burnham, ed., *Postmodern Theology: Christian Faith in a Pluralist World* (San Francisco: Harper, 1989), and Stanley J. Grenz, *A Primer on Postmodernism* (Grand Rapids: Eerdmans, 1996).

9. Miroslav Volf, *Exclusion and Embrace: A Theological Exploration of Identity, Otherness, and Reconciliation* (Nashville: Abingdon, 1996), 106.

10. Robert Bellah, *Habits of the Heart: Individualism and Commitment in American Life* (Berkeley: University of California Press, 1985), 152–155.

11. James F. Hopewell, *Congregation: Stories and Structures* (Philadelphia: Fortress, 1987), 58–62.

12. Jane Smiley, *A Thousand Acres* (New York: Ivy, 1991), 225, 227.

13. Conveyed by the Reverend Greg Schrimpf in a class discussion.

14. Theissen, *Social Setting*, 107.

Chapter 6

1. For a helpful overview, see Margaret M. Mitchell, *Paul and the Rhetoric of Reconciliation: An Exegetical Investigation of the Language and Composition of 1 Corinthians* (Louisville: Westminster/John Knox, 1991), 157–164.

2. Ibid., 92–96.

3. Ibid., 158.

4. Note what appears to be an intentional omission of the male/female pair found in Galatians 3:28. Is Paul wary of mentioning this pair in light of his debates with the women at Corinth (7:1–16; 11:2–16)?

5. James L. Bailey and Lyle D. Vander Broek, *Literary Forms in the New Testament: A Handbook* (Louisville: Westminster/John Knox, 1992), 76–77.

6. It is quite possible that the Corinthians believed their gift of tongues was a dialect of the angels, as in *Testament of Job*, 48–50; see Gordon Fee, *The First Epistle to the Corinthians* (Grand Rapids: Eerdmans, 1987), 630.

7. Bailey and Vander Broek, *Literary Forms*, 49–54.

8. Dale Martin, *The Corinthian Body* (New Haven: Yale University Press, 1995), 87ff.

9. Ibid., 96.

10. Ibid., 101.

11. See Fee, *First Epistle*, 699–708.

12. Bailey and Vander Broek, *Literary Forms*, 58–59.

13. Robert J. Banks, *Paul's Idea of Community: The Early House Churches in Their Historical Setting* (Grand Rapids: Eerdmans, 1980), 102–103.

14. John W. De Gruchy, *Christianity and Democracy: A Theology for a Just World Order*, Cambridge: Cambridge University Press, 1995), 240–241.

15. Dietrich Bonhoeffer, *Letters and Papers from Prison*, ed. Eberhard Bethge (London: SCM Press, 1953), 162–174; see comments by John W. De Gruchy, *Christianity, Art, and Transformation: Theological Aesthetics in the Struggle for Justice* (Cambridge: Cambridge University Press, 2001), 158–162.

16. Bonhoeffer, *Letters and Papers*, 162–163.

17. Caroline J. Simon, *The Disciplined Heart: Love, Destiny, and Imagination* (Grand Rapids: Eerdmans, 1997), 28.

18. Miroslav Volf, *Exclusion and Embrace: A Theological Exploration of Identity, Otherness, and Reconciliation* (Nashville: Abingdon, 1996), 250–253.

19. William M. Easum, *Sacred Cows Make Gourmet Burgers: Ministry Anytime, Anywhere, by Anybody* (Nashville: Abingdon, 1995).

Chapter 7

1. From Menander's work *Thais*. Menander (342–291 B.C.E.) was a popular Greek dramatist. The line Paul quotes was probably a common saying in his day.

2. James L. Bailey and Lyle D. Vander Broek, *Literary Forms in the New Testament: A Handbook* (Louisville: Westminster/John Knox, 1992), 38–41.

3. Dale Martin, *The Corinthian Body* (New Haven: Yale University Press, 1995), chapter 5, "The Resurrected Body."

4. Martin, *Corinthian Body*, 109–113.

5. Martin, *Corinthian Body*, 114–116.

6. Martin points to Lucian's *Lover of Lies* as a good source for such tales (*Corinthian Body*, 112). Especially common are instances of magicians raising the dead for short terms and for specific "assignments," not at all unlike what we have seen in popular interpretations of Caribbean Vodun (Voodoo).

7. Martin, *Corinthian Body*, chapter 5.